THE LEXILE FRAMEWORK: AN INTRODUCTION FOR EDUCATORS

by

Thomas Schnick

&

Mark J. Knickelbine

Foreword by A.J. Stenner

ACKNOWLEDGEMENTS

We owe a debt of thanks to the many people who contributed their efforts to the production and publication of this book. For instance, our proofreading and prepress gurus, Debra Lovelien, Sandee Horn, and Lissa Gottwals, all spent spent untold hours refining the copy. Our primary reviewers, Steve Davis and Ellie Sanford, provided valuable insights for the professional content review. And thanks also to Robert Meyer, without whose assistance this book could not have been produced. Each of these firms also provided significant assistance during the creation of this book:

EBSCO Publishing

Follett Software Company

NoveList

Sagebrush Learning Resources

Table of Contents

FOREWORD

When Malbert Smith, my other colleagues, and I were researching and developing the Lexile Framework, we dreamed of creating a kind of universal language that educators, students, parents, and researchers could use to talk about reading. Today, with major book publishers listing Lexile measures on their books, major test publishers reporting results in Lexiles, and more than 10 million students nationwide involved in Lexile-linked reading programs, our dream is becoming a reality. We are well on our way to becoming the standard by which reading comprehension and text difficulty are measured.

We realize, however, that it is not enough simply to develop Lexile-based tools. For the potential of *The Lexile Framework for Reading®* to be realized, these tools have to be used effectively by educators who understand them and who value their potential to promote reading success for students. This book was written to introduce educators, especially those who teach and foster literacy, to the Lexile Framework, and to provide them with the basic information they need to begin implementing this vital new tool in their classrooms, libraries, and communities.

The key to the promise of the Lexile Framework is its ability to place students and texts on a common scale. With Lexile-linked reading comprehension tests on one hand, and Lexile-based book leveling and reading lists on the other, we have both assessments and instructional tools that are calibrated in the same manner. In this way, the Lexile Framework brings instruction and assessment together, two worlds that in the past have been all too separate.

This assessment-instruction link enables educators to target reading experiences for students in a way that will help them find reading to be a much more enjoyable and valuable experience. Teachers and administrators often talk about the need for more individualized instruction. Between test results on the Lexile scale and Lexiled texts, teachers, students, and parents can, at last, prepare a reading enrichment program based on hard, scientific evidence.

In some respects, what we are doing is nothing new. Methods for determining the readability of texts have existed for more than 70 years, and there are a variety of such tools in use today. However, the Lexile Framework represents a significant shift over past efforts in three main ways:

- The readability analysis of texts is based on the entire text of each book or document. Every word is counted; every sentence length is measured. Many other readability formulas are based only on samples from a text;
- Individual reading ability is measured through tests that correspond to the same scale, solving the "apples-and-oranges" problem of trying to convert test scores into grade equivalents;
- Because it can be linked to any text and any reading assessment, the Lexile Framework is an open system that can be applied universally wherever the English language is written and read.

One way to think of the Lexile Framework is to think of a thermometer. Temperature is generally measured on one of two scales, Celsius or Fahrenheit. Each is an absolute scale, and I can determine the temperature equivalent on each based on a formula. I can then use that temperature to make decisions—whether my child has a fever, or how I should dress to go outside.

By being able to measure the reading comprehension of students individually and putting them on the same scale with reading material—almost any material, from textbooks to comic books—we can estimate the degree of reading challenge appropriate for any student in any given situation. We can avoid overwhelming readers with material that is too difficult for them to cope with, and we can avoid boring readers with reading that does not provide enough challenge to stimulate curiosity and promote reading motivation.

As we learn more about reading engagement, it is clear that this kind of targeting is essential to motivate student reading, enhance students' sense of mastery and self-direction, and promote the development of decoding, comprehension, and thinking skills. But just as a thermometer won't cure your cold, the Lexile Framework in and of itself will not cure a student's reading problems. The Lexile Framework is only valuable in the hands of skilled educators who know how to use the information it provides, in combination with their other observations and assessments, to create an environment that fosters each student's literacy growth.

A Summary of the Book

Here is a brief introduction to the main points made in *The Lexile Framework: An Introduction for Educators:*

An important key to reading development is reading engagement. In turn, reading engagement requires that students feel a sense of mastery over text. As educators, we cannot leave this experience of mastery to chance; we must guide students to reading experiences that provide appropriate degrees of challenge.

The common practice of matching students with texts on the basis of grade levels drawn from standardized tests and readability formulas is flawed, because these instruments and formulas do not use a common, absolute scale to measure text readability or student reading ability.

By contrast, The Lexile Framework provides an absolute, equal-interval scale to measure readability. A "Lexile" is a standard unit for measuring the comprehensibility of a text. Furthermore, when we know the Lexile measure of text that a student can comprehend, we can also assign a Lexile measure to the student. Thus, both student ability and text difficulty may be placed on a common scale, allowing educators to make easy and accurate decisions as to the level of reading challenge most appropriate for a student.

A student's Lexile measure is set at the level of text the student can read with 75 percent comprehension; it corresponds to an instructional reading level for the student. This means that the student's Lexile measure marks a point in a reading range than extends about 50 Lexiles above and 100 Lexiles below the student measure.

While the Lexile Analyzer can be used to measure the readability of text, a variety of factors will influence the level of challenge a student perceives in any reading situation: the reader's background, motivations and expectations; generic aspects of the text itself; and the environmental context in which the reading takes place. When the teacher knows a student's Lexile reading range, he or she can compensate for reader, text and context factors by guiding students to materials that match the higher or lower segments of the student's range.

Because the Lexile scale is absolute, it can be applied to any student, nearly all texts, and most reading assessments, including informal assessments and observations made by the teacher. The Lexile scale gives us a way to combine our assessments of student reading, providing a source of multiple indicators to enrich our understanding of student ability and growth.

All of these factors make the Lexile Framework a particularly versatile tool for educators to apply in many school- and home-based reading programs. Reading teachers may use it to set and track goals for independent reading; content teachers can use Lexile ranges to compensate for disparities between student reading comprehension levels and the readability of assigned texts. If students or teachers wish to use texts that are above the student's Lexile range, a number of scaffolding techniques may be needed to help students negotiate the texts successfully.

Lexiles may be used along with computerized reading management programs to provide students with added motivation and give teachers multiple indicators of student ability and progress.

The Lexile Framework can help librarians and media specialists guide student reading selections, develop library collections, and collaborate with classroom teachers.

Because Lexiles relate easily to actual texts, educators can use the Lexile Framework to set reading standards and benchmarks, and to facilitate communication about reading issues with parents and the public at large.

Chapter One, The Dynamics of Reading Engagement, is an overview of The Lexile Framework for Reading and is essential reading for all educators interested in learning about the framework.

Chapter Four explains the psychometric theory and research related to the development of the Lexile Framework. This overview was written for researchers and educators who want to learn more about the finer points of measuring a student's reading abilities and text readability.

Chapters Two and Three and Five through Seven were written for teachers and educators who are involved in the process of guiding students to appropriate reading choices. Chapter Two provides a framework for matching readers with texts that considers the relationships between the reader, the text, and the context. Chapter Three, The Lexile Framework—A Common Metric, explains how the Lexile Framework works and how to target readers to text. Chapters Five and Six introduce the reader to using the Lexile Framework in common reading situations and how to moderate text difficulty depending on the ability of the reader. In addition, suggestions for using the Lexile Framework to reinforce familiar content material to enhance the learning of new concepts are presented. Chapter Seven discusses the role of the Lexile Framework in the media center and how to help students make informed choices when selecting texts to read. Chapter Eight, Using Lexiles with Reading Management Systems, discusses how the Lexile Framework can be used in conjunction with instructional management systems (IMS) software. This chapter was written for educators interested in the fundamentals of computer-assisted learning and the available software.

Chapter Nine discusses the role of communication in systemic reform and how the common language of the Lexile Framework can enhance this communication. This chapter is essential reading for all educators, especially those in high-stakes accountability situations.

Equity and excellence in schools have been policy goals for many years. During the 1990s, educational reform debates have centered on the notion that the way to achieve equity and excellence in our schools is through increased accountability. The result has been the adoption of challenging standards about what students are expected to know and be able to do. Chapter Ten describes how the Lexile Framework can be used to establish, monitor, evaluate, and discuss reading performance standards. This chapter was written for educators interested in using the Lexile Framework for accountability purposes.

Tom Schnick and Mark Knickelbine have done an admirable job of creating a basic handbook that will help teachers, reading specialists, and library media specialists discover the tremendous potential of Lexiles, and begin to put that potential to use to help each of their students become the best readers they can be. My hope is that, by allowing educators to add the Lexile Framework to their pedagogical toolbox, the publication of this book will be one more step toward helping every child discover the power and joy of literacy.

A. J. Stenner

Chairman

MetaMetrics, Inc.

CHAPTER 1

THE DYNAMICS OF READING ENGAGEMENT

The results of the 1998 reading assessment conducted by the National Assessment of Educational Progress should be sobering for every educator. While modest statistical gains were made overall, the results suggest that the reading skills of American intermediate and secondary school children have not improved markedly in more than 20 years. Twenty-two percent of high school seniors who took the exam failed to reach the level of basic reading competency. And results continue to be worse for poor children, members of ethnic minorities, and students in urban schools.

As Snow, Burns and Griffin (1998) pointed out in a review of similar results from the 1996 NAEP tests, American students do well in reading compared to children worldwide. But do they do well enough? Snow concludes:

> ...[T]he educational careers of 25 to 40 percent of American children are imperiled because they do not read well enough, quickly enough or easily enough to ensure comprehension in their content courses in middle and secondary school. Although some men and women with reading disability can and do attain significant levels of academic and occupational achievement, more typically poor readers, unless strategic interventions in reading are afforded them, fare poorly on the educational and, subsequently, the occupational ladder. Although difficult to translate into actual dollar amounts, the costs to society are probably quite high in terms of lower productivity, underemployment, mental health services, and other measures.

As we might expect, when students find reading difficult, they read less, and it's clear that students' distaste for reading grows as they get older. According to NAEP, the proportion of students who report reading for fun almost every day drops by nearly half between fourth and twelfth grades, from 45 percent to 24 percent. At the same time, the proportion of students who report never or hardly ever reading for fun more than doubles, from 12 to 27 percent (NAEP, 1998).

These statistics are troubling, because we know from both research and our personal experience as educators that the amount of time students spend reading has a direct impact on their reading ability and development. Reading is a set of skills, and, as with any other skill, continual practice is required to maintain and grow in proficiency. "Practice makes perfect," we say, and the following research bears out our folk wisdom:

- Students who report reading outside school activities every day score 21 to 29 points higher on the National Assessment of Educational Progress reading test than students who seldom do such reading (NAEP, 1998).
- NAEP scores also demonstrate that students who read 11 or more pages for school demonstrate above-average reading ability; those who read 5 or fewer pages perform below average (NAEP 1998).
- Numerous studies have demonstrated that reading practice has a powerful effect on student reading fluency and vocabulary growth (Krashen, 1992).
- Frequent readers develop a more robust store of various kinds of content knowledge as well—200 to 400% higher levels of content knowledge than less frequent and active readers (Cunningham and Stanovich, 1998).

Researchers also reveal the reverse effect: Struggling readers read less and less, resulting in limited vocabulary growth and reading development (Walberg, et al. 1984; Walberg and Tsai, 1993). This lack of skills, combined with the experience of associating reading with feelings of failure, further decreases student motivation to read (Stanovich, 1986).

The harmful impact of this downward spiral is evident to classroom teachers in the upper grades. Because students can't or won't do assigned reading, teachers find that they cannot use textbooks as effective learning tools. As a result, they either assume students are not doing assigned reading and rely on lecture to fill in the gap, or they simply stop giving reading assignments altogether. This abandonment of textbooks not only robs classrooms of one of their most effective learning tools; it also reinforces the downward spiral of reading by removing yet another opportunity for reading practice.

It is little wonder, then, that outside the school walls we are seeing an increasing number of people who are functionally illiterate. While the reading scores of 12th graders have remained relatively static over the years, the level of literacy required in our high-tech workplaces has increased dramatically. Beyond the growing divide between reading ability and reading demands is the phenomenon of aliteracy: people who can read, but who choose not to, and rely instead on a passive, oral means of information and entertainment—television.

The story is clear: As individuals read more, they become better readers. As they read less, their reading skills fail to develop and literacy becomes less and less relevant to them. Is there anything that we as educators can do to give students a better start? What can we do to make their early practice more successful for them, so that they will enjoy reading more, and, as a result, read more—reaping as they do a wealth of benefits, both in school and in life? What can we do to help students not only learn to read, but also to become engaged readers?

Reading Engagement

The research of Sweet and Guthrie (1994) into teachers' perceptions of reading motivation supports a common observation: Some students seem disposed to be "immersed" or "engrossed" in reading, while others do not. This kind of intense motivation is associated with reading engagement, an active orientation to text that finds its source in the personal desires and purposes of the reader. As Guthrie and Alverman (1999) observe:

> Active reading is grounded in intrinsic motivations. It is common sense that people read for a reason. Reading is a conscious, deliberate act prompted by a plausible purpose. When an individual's reasons for reading include curiosity, the desire for aesthetic involvement, or the disposition for social interchange, that individual is likely to be an active reader...Students who want to read for personally significant reasons will invest time in reading. Our view is that engagement in reading is a motivated mental activity with vital consequences for world knowledge and social participation (p. 17).

The key to reading engagement, then, is to help each student discover literacy as a means of fulfilling one's desires, of achieving one's purposes, and of satisfying one's curiosity. If we can assume that all children have desires and purposes, then our primary goal as reading teachers must be to facilitate the student's ability to recognize and apply the tools of literacy to their individual motivations. We must do more than provide reading instruction, reading materials, and reading time; we must ensure that students have successful experiences with text. A second grader who loves trucks, but is unable to read books about trucks that are displayed in his classroom, has missed an opportunity to internalize the link between literacy and personal fulfillment. We would venture to guess that it is a history of such lost opportunities that leads to the declining interest in reading we see in students as they grow older—and that a "gifted reader" may often be one for whom the link between reading and personal need satisfaction was forged and reinforced from an early age.

The key to building reading engagement, then, is to help students recognize reading as a means of need fulfillment and to foster the initial and ongoing successes that will reinforce literacy as a self-motivated strategy for learning, aesthetic pleasure, and social interaction. How are we as teachers to structure such reading experiences for our students? Besides understanding the personal motivations of our students, we must understand how the relationship between personal ability and text challenge affects reading motivation.

Reading as a "Flow" Experience

Think about the most exhilarating moments of your life—winning a challenging game, acing a tough assignment, victoriously pushing yourself to new achievements. Whatever your peak experiences have been, chances are they shared certain key characteristics:

- You were completely absorbed and almost effortlessly focused on what you were doing;
- You had a sense of mastering a new challenge, a sense that your personal boundaries were expanding and your competency was growing;
- You were tremendously motivated by the experience, and drawn to try to repeat it as often as you could.

University of Chicago psychologist Michael Csikszentmihali (1991) studied such optimal experiences for more than 20 years, experiences in which people felt a sense of profound self-confidence and sense of mastery in their work or play, in which their concentration and ability seemed to "flow." Csikszentmihali discovered that this "flow state" was associated with learning, higher-order thinking development, and profound intrinsic motivation. Nearly any kind of activity can provide the conditions for the flow state—even academic tasks. In fact, one of the most common flow experiences is that of being completely engaged in a rewarding book—"being lost in your reading."

As a teacher, you have probably experienced this kind of deep engagement with reading many times, and the kind of experience you want your students to discover as well. In fact, it is useful to think about the kind of self-motivated, self-directed reading, thinking, and learning we want our students to develop as the kind of flow state that Csikszentmihali describes.

Finding the Flow

Csikszentmihali uses a simple graph to demonstrate an important factor in creating the conditions under which optimal experiences occur (Figure 1). The graph plots the perceived difficulty of any task against the self-perceived competence of the individual doing the task.

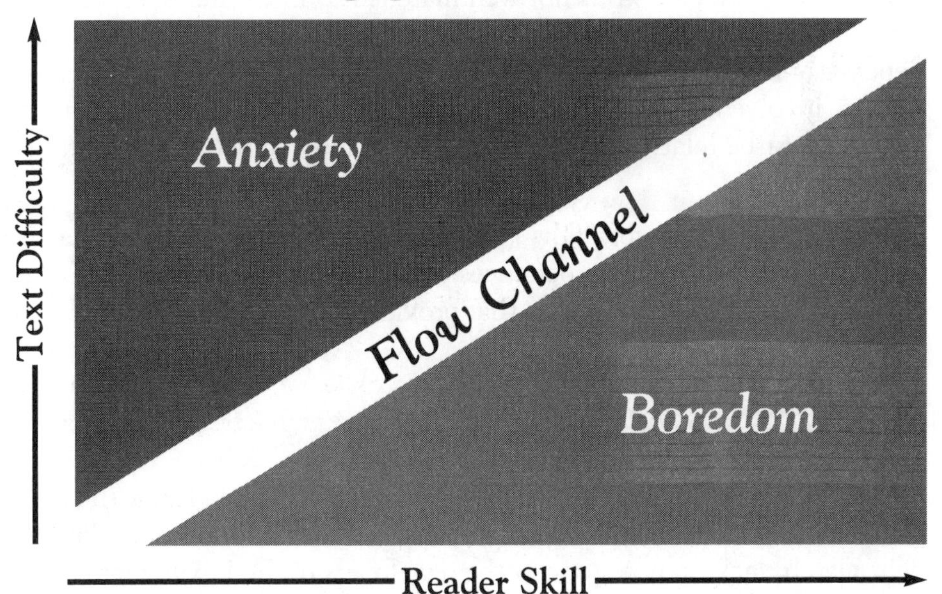

Fig 1

When the difficulty of a task is greater than our ability—real or perceived—to perform it, we experience anxiety. If the task is too easy for us, we are likely to be bored and find it difficult to pay attention or become fully engaged in a task. However, when the difficulty of the task is properly balanced with our competence, conditions are right for us to experience the motivation and growth of the "flow" experience.

Reading teachers will immediately recognize the dynamics of these ideas in the students they have taught. They have witnessed the paralyzing fear of a child who is convinced he cannot read an assigned passage, and the restless boredom of the reader who has grown beyond the difficulty of the assignment. In fact, reading researchers Reed and Schallert (1993) have usefully applied Csikszentmihali's flow concept to the challenge of reading engagement.

If a reader believes the text to be beyond his or her capabilities, he or she may not devote the necessary amount of attention to it; instead the reader may experience anxiety about how he or she will make sense of the text while worrying about how to approach the task. Conversely, if a text appears too easy, the reader may not choose to devote the necessary amount of attention to it, believing that his or her attention can be divided between it and other tasks.

If a reader views a text as not well matched to his or her abilities, Reed and Schallert speculate, he or she may react negatively to the author, experiencing annoyance, anxiety, indignation, or boredom. Because readers who are involved in a text are wholly focused on their tasks, their approach to texts must be relatively free of extraneous and competing thoughts and emotions.

Creating conditions for "flow" state in reading, then, requires that we guide students to reading experiences which balance the student's reading ability and confidence with texts that provide the appropriate level of challenge for the given reading purpose.

"Fifth-Grade Shoes"

With the critical importance of matching developing readers with appropriate reading challenge, it's clear we need a better method of finding the right match. Jack Stenner, one of the developers of the Lexile Framework, tells this story about an unsuccessful hunt for shoes and books.

> Some time ago I went into a shoe store and asked for a fifth-grade shoe. The clerk looked at me suspiciously and asked if I knew how much shoe sizes varied among eleven-year-olds. Furthermore, he pointed out that shoe size was not nearly as important as purpose, style, color, and so on. But if I would specify the features I wanted and the size, he could walk to the back and quickly reappear with several options to my liking. He further noted, somewhat condescendingly, that the store used the same metric to measure feet and shoes, and when there was a match between foot and shoe, the shoes got worn, there was no pain, the customer was happy and became a repeat customer. I called home and got my son's shoe size

> and then asked the clerk for a size 8, red, high-top, Penny Hardaway basketball shoe. After a brief transaction I had the shoes.
>
> I then walked next door to my favorite bookstore and asked for a fifth-grade fantasy novel. Without hesitation, the clerk led me to a shelf where she gave me three choices. I selected one and went home with *The Hobbit,* a classic that I had read three times myself as a youngster. My son, I later learned, had yet to achieve the reading fluency needed to enjoy *The Hobbit.* His understandable response to my gift was to put the book down in favor of passionately practicing free-throws in the driveway.

This parable is an amusing story that's based on a very serious problem. Of course we wouldn't think of asking a sales clerk at a shoe store for a "fifth-grade" shoe, because we know that a child's grade in school has little relevance to the size and kind of shoe she needs. Each succeeding report of NAEP reading test results, along with our own experience as educators, provides us with ample evidence that the individual reading ability of children in a given school grade can vary just as much as their shoe sizes. Yet we continue to use clumsy grade-leveling methods to match children with books, and scratch our heads when our students find the resulting "fit" a painful one (Stenner, 1999).

What educators need, and what they have lacked until now, is the same kind of tool the shoe store clerk has. Just as shoe sizes apply to both shoes and feet, we need a metric that can be applied to both reader and text. And just as a shoe clerk needs a metric for size, we need a metric that applies specifically to reading comprehension levels—not age, grade level, or any other factor that may have only an indirect connection to what we want to measure.

This book will provide you with tools that will give you new insights into guiding all students to the reading experiences that are right for them. It will introduce you to The Lexile Framework® for Reading, a new and powerful tool for determining the reading ability of students and finding texts that provide the appropriate level of challenge. It will also show you how to combine the information Lexiles provide with other sources of information, such as comprehension tests, interest inventories, reading logs, and your own observations and experiences, to give students proper reading guidance in a wide variety of reading situations.

Conclusion

Guiding students to engaging and rewarding reading experiences can be a complicated task. Many factors are involved in matching each student with his or her individual learning style, background, and developmental level, with the ever-expanding universe of texts for young people. Yet the more we learn about literacy development, the more we are convinced that the individual guidance of teachers to literacy experiences is a vital part of every child's reading development.

References

Csikszentmihali, M. (1991). Literacy and intrinsic motivation. In S. Graubard (Ed.), *Literacy: An overview by fourteen experts* (pp. 115-140). New York: The Noonday Press.

Csikszentmihali, M., & Csikszentmihali, I. (1988). *Optimal experience: Psychological studies of flow in consciousness.* New York: Cambridge University Press.

Cunningham, A.E., & Stanovich, K.E. (1998). What reading does for the mind. *American Educator,* Spring/Summer, 8-15.

Guthrie, J., & Alverman, D. (1999). *Engaged reading: Processes, practices and policy implications.* New York: Teachers College Press.

Krashen, S. (1993). *The power of reading: Insights from the research.* Englewood, CO: Libraries Unlimited, Inc.

National Assessment of Educational Progress. (1999). *NAEP 1998 Reading Report Card for the Nation and the States.* Washington, D.C.: National Center for Education Statistics.

Reed, J., & Schallert, D. (1993). The nature of involvement in academic discourse tasks. *Journal of Educational Psychology,* 85, 253-266.

Snow, C., Burns, S., & Griffin, P. (1998). *Preventing reading difficulties in young children.* Washington, D.C.: National Academy Press.

Stanovich, K.E. (1986). Matthew effects in reading: Some consequences of individual differences in the acquisition of literacy. *Reading Research Quarterly,* 21, 360-407.

Stenner, A. J. (1999). *Matching students to text: The targeted reader.* New York: Scholastic Center for Literacy & Learning.

Sweet, A., & Guthrie, J. (1994). *Teacher perceptions of students' motivations to read* (Reading Research Report No. 29). Athens, GA: Universities of Georgia and Maryland, National Reading Research Center.

Walberg, H.J., Strykowski, B.R., Royal, E., & Hung, S.S. (1984). Exceptional performance. *Review of Educational Research,* 54, 87-112.

Walberg, H.J., & Tsai, S. (1983). Matthew effects in education. *American Educational Research Journal,* 20, 359-373.

CHAPTER 2

MATCHING READERS AND TEXTS

Introduction

While the Lexile Framework provides an improved tool for determining reading ability and text difficulty, guiding a student to appropriate reading choices is never as simple as matching two numbers. As with the many reading-related metrics already available—test scores, percentiles, readability formulas, and the like—there is always the danger that we can begin to think of measuring student reading ability to be like measuring rainwater in a tube. Because the numbers we work with have the appearance of hard, objective facts, we begin to think of reading comprehension as something tangible that exists in a reader's head.

But saying that a student reads at a 4.6 grade level, or at the 67th percentile, or even at 850L, is not the same as saying that a student is 38 inches tall. As we will discuss, the instruments we use to measure student reading comprehension can only give us an approximation of the student's ability on the day he or she was tested—to say nothing of weeks or months after the test. Beyond that, the student's ability to successfully use text depends on many environmental factors that go beyond the semantic and syntactic difficulty of the text itself.

Before we discuss The Lexile Framework® for Reading and its uses in the next chapter, first it will be useful for us to consider the various challenges before us when guiding students to reading materials that best suit their needs.

The Teacher as Guide

Experienced reading teachers know that creating such a balance between text difficulty and reader competence is more difficult than the apparent simplicity of Csikszentmihali's flow graph might lead one to believe. While especially true for emerging readers, students at all levels need the teacher to serve as a literate, experienced guide who can help them negotiate the many decisions that must be made when choosing a text, whether for learning or sheer enjoyment. More importantly, as fewer children have the advantages of a literacy-rich home environment, the responsibility of the teacher to help make the student's initial experiences with reading rewarding and successful cannot be underestimated.

Some school reading decisions are already made for students and teachers: the adoption of course materials, for instance. However, the more reading and learning are viewed as individualized processes, the more individual decisions need to be made about books and other texts. Older students may have a greater awareness of the difficulty of print materials than some younger students; nevertheless, even secondary students are not usually as knowledgeable about language difficulty and other kinds of text challenges as the teacher may be. The teacher who artfully guides student choices will teach students valuable skills for making informed choices themselves.

Due to time constraints and the nature of some assignments, the teacher sometimes chooses books for students. At other times, students may read freely, choosing their own materials and reading at their own pace. Most often, however, the process of selecting books and supplementary materials is best done as a shared process, the teacher serving as a guide to help students find the texts that reflect their interests and meet their developmental needs. Shared literacy decisions fulfill the model of language development proposed by Vygotsky (1978), in which the teacher is the literate coach, leading developing readers along the path to proficiency.

Factors to Consider

The following format, adapted from the Wisconsin Department of Public Instruction's *Guide to Curriculum Planning in Reading* (Cook, 1986) lists a variety of factors we need to consider when matching students with appropriate tasks. Each factor can affect the competency of the reader and/or the difficulty of the reading task, whether real or perceived. As we consider these factors, we should remember two important aspects of the conditions that lead to the flow state:

- The balance point between difficulty and competence is dynamic, changing constantly with different tasks and the passage of time. Making the match is not a static process of labeling students and books, but an ongoing developmental process in which the various factors are seldom in the same alignment twice.
- Rather than seek some absolute value that tells us either student ability or text difficulty, we should remember that it is the stu-

dent's perception about the difficulty of the text that is most important. If a third-grader is daunted by reading chapter books, the fact that her reading test scores match the readability of the text will not matter to her! We must be concerned with the student's level of self-confidence and awareness of her own capabilities as well as with her intellectual development.

The Reader

The individual needs, perceptions and background of the reader are of paramount importance.

- **Background of Experience**—Each student will come to class with a unique history that defines her expectations about literacy: the extent to which books are shared at home, the importance that adults and peers place on literacy, the cultural surroundings in which literacy experiences take place. Together, these expectations will determine a student's attitudes toward a particular reading assignment.
- **Knowledge of Subject**—The student's familiarity and interest in the subject matter will have a powerful influence on his perceived ability to handle a particular text.
- **Vocabulary**—With varied histories and bases of knowledge, students will have developed a wide range of different vocabularies. The student will be more comfortable and successful with material that supports her individual vocabulary development.
- **Developmental Level**—Beyond the traditional tested reading level derived from a student's test scores, we must also be concerned with emotional development. A gifted third-grader may not be ready for Young Adult literature, even as his less-fluent peer may be bored with primers or picture books.
- **Purpose and Motivation**—Why is the student reading? Is she seeking an engaging or pleasurable experience, or searching for relevant and important information? Or is she completing an assignment or seeking to meet the external expectations of her school or home environment? Understanding what the reading experience means to the student is the most crucial factor in guiding that student to appropriate texts.

The Text

Once we understand the student and his needs, we can evaluate any given text by whether it reflects the background, interests, and motivations of the student.

- Is the content consistent with the student's background and reading purpose?
- Does the format of the book add or detract from its perceived difficulty? This is an especially important consideration as children transition from picture books to chapter books, or as they are introduced to reference works, nonfiction, or classic literature.

Is the linguistic difficulty appropriate for the student's needs? How should linguistic difficulty be adjusted in light of the other kinds of challenges this text presents to the student? As we will discuss, making this kind of adjustment is a recurring challenge for teachers.

- Concept Difficulty—The student may be able to decode the text, but does he or she have the background and developmental maturity to make sense of the concepts?
- The work's organization may present additional challenges, especially as students search for specific information in reference or nonfiction books.
- Author's Purpose—Does the "virtual audience" the author had in mind have the same background, needs, and level of development as the student? Mismatches here could increase or diminish the perceived difficulty of the text.

The Context

While we are often silently concentrating on a book in front of us, reading is actually a social process. What we find motivating or worrying, valuable or useless is determined by our involvement with the people around us; our self-image is determined by how we see ourselves reflected in the eyes of others.

- Setting is extremely important. For any given student, the classroom, home, library or reading area each present a unique set of challenges.
- Task—How does the student interpret your expectations of the reading assignment? If we think of the different mindset a student

will bring to free reading of story literature as compared with doing research for a term project, we can understand that the nature of the task involved impact the student's perceived competence.

- Objectives and Outcomes—There are often explicit objectives and outcomes set by the teacher or curriculum; in addition there may be many unstated expectations about what and how the student is to perform. All of these will have an impact on the appropriateness of a given text.

Guiding students to appropriate text selections is a multilayered process that involves numerous tangible and intangible factors that must be harmonized. While the complexity of the process may appear daunting, there are techniques available to teachers that can help make the process easier and more successful for both teacher and student.

The Challenge of Matching

Observe an experienced reading teacher at work with one of her children, and you will discover that the most common way teachers guide student book selection is by using their own experienced judgment. By listening to students read aloud, an experienced teacher can spot the more advanced readers as well as the less proficient among the class. Indeed, the intuition born of personal experience will always be the teacher's first and most important tool for guiding students.

However, most teachers also feel that their own judgment is not sufficient. It takes considerable teaching experience to develop the kind of informed judgment that can take the unusual into account as well as the commonplace. As objective as one may try to be, the possibility for biased or mistaken judgments exists. And knowing every student, to say nothing of the overwhelming amount of material available for student reading, is a daunting challenge at best. Research shows that teacher judgments of the relative difficulty of textual materials can vary by as much as six grade levels (Jorgenson, 1977).

Experienced teachers who know their students and the material at hand will be able to distinguish between easy readers, intermediate books, and difficult reading consistently and with accuracy. To test yourself, place the following books in their order of difficulty, from easiest to hardest:

Henry and Mudge and the Wild Wind
If You Please, President Lincoln
Moby Dick
Nate the Great
The Hobbit

You were probably certain, or at least reasonably confident, that this list of books should be ranked in this order of difficulty:

Nate the Great (130L)
Henry and Mudge and the Wild Wind (400L)
If You Please, President Lincoln (720L)
The Hobbit (1000L)
Moby Dick (1200L)

Using our experience and judgment to rank order different books becomes more difficult when we have to compare titles that are similar, such as books by the same author or social studies textbooks that are all written for the same grade level. For example, try to place these books in their order of difficulty, from easiest to hardest:

The Adventures of Tom Sawyer
Every Living Thing
A Connecticut Yankee in King Arthur's Court
Pudd'nhead Wilson
The Prince and the Pauper

Perhaps you realized that these books are already in the correct order of difficulty (900L, 1000L, 1050L, 1130L, and 1160L, respectively). No doubt you also realized that this exercise wasn't nearly as easy to complete as the first. When textual materials are written at roughly the same level, it's much more difficult for even experienced teachers to rank them in order of difficulty. Unfortunately, of the two examples, it is the second that comes closest to our daily experience working with children and texts.

It is no wonder, then, that teachers have traditionally relied on a variety of tools to help verify their own judgment and help ascertain both student ability and text difficulty. The tools most commonly relied upon are leveling formulas for text difficulty. While these tools can provide useful information, they can at times make it difficult for teachers to obtain, understand, and use the information they generate to help match students with appropriate materials.

Reading Tests

Norm-referenced interpretations of traditional standardized reading tests identify a student's reading achievement in relation to other students who take the same test. If a fourth grader scores in the 70th percentile on a particular test, it means that he reads better than 69 percent of the other fourth graders who took the same test. Such test results are then often convertible to grade equivalencies, which tend to be the basic unit on which text-matching decisions are made.

All measuremments contain some error—whether it arises from the selection of questions that were asked, the conditions under which the test was administered, or the motivation of the test-taker. In reading, where skill development tends to change at a smaller rate as the reader matures, this measurement error in a specific test score can be as much as the average difference between two grade levels. A single test score only provides an estimate of the student's ability on that day with those questions. For a more accurate understanding of the student's actual ability, multiple measures and sources of information should always be employed when making decisions that affect individuals.

Teachers often state that the difficulty of administering these tests and the long time it takes to receive the results often make them a poor source of information for text matching. In addition, the basic information the tests do provide is a comparison of a student's performance with the body of other students taking the exam; they say little about what the individual student can achieve or ought to be able to achieve. Finally, the test is a snapshot of student performance on one day and, therefore, cannot provide the ongoing information about student development teachers find most helpful.

Readability Scales

There are a variety of formulas available that can report the comprehension level of texts, typically reported in terms of grade equivalents. Traditional readability formulas are all based on a simple theory about written language and use relatively simple equations to calculate text difficulty. There are currently more than 50 such formulas in use. While each has discrete features, nearly all attempt to assign difficulty based on a combination of vocabulary and sentence length (Klare, 1974).

If you took any ten books and compared their ratings on the various readability formulas, you would discover that most formulas agree on how to rank the books in order of their difficulty. You would also discover, however, that the various formulas disagree about the actual grade level rating of any given book—sometimes widely.

While one can debate the relative accuracy of one readability formula compared to others, they are all based on simple mathematical equations that attempt to model the difficulty of written language; there is no ideal (error-free) measure of text difficulty against which they can be judged.

The Apples and Oranges Problem

With test scores and readability formula in hand, teachers frequently attempt to match children with books, usually based on some grade level determination. So, for instance, if a student's test score suggests they read at a fourth-grade level, the teacher will look for books ranked at a fourth-grade level by the readability formula. In some instances, these formulas can be used to break down grade equivalencies in tenths of a year, a calibration some teachers take quite seriously in guiding student reading.

Our discussion above, however, shows that there are some significant problems with this approach. Test scores are based on norms of student achievement; readability formulas are based on mathematical equations that model language difficulty. In short, there is no real relationship between a grade equivalency determined from a test score and one determined from a readability formula. Even though both appear to be giving the same kind of information, both are based on entirely different kinds of measurement.

Given the measurement error of reading test scores and the disagreement among readability formulas as to grade ratings for specific books, it is clear that this method, as widespread as it may be, is really quite an unreliable method of determining which texts are appropriate for a given student in a given situation. It is no wonder, then, that teachers we talk to are dissatisfied with the tools they have traditionally used to judge student ability and text difficulty.

Grade Equivalent (GE) Scores

Grade Equivalent (GE) scores are commonly used to compare individual student performance on standardized achievement tests with those of a norm group. A GE score consists of a whole number and a tenth to represent a portion of the year. For example, a GE of 5.1 is equivalent to an average raw score corresponding to the fifth grade, first month of school. GEs are popular because many teachers and parents believe they are easy to understand.

However, although they seem intuitive, GEs are very easily misinterpreted and often assumed to correlate directly to readability grade levels. Interpreting GEs correctly requires a thorough understanding of the scale's construction.

The underlying GE scale is a complex, non-linear function that is only loosely tied to the normative data. In fact it is a statistical model constructed from the 50th percentile point (the median raw score average) corresponding to each grade (Figure 2).

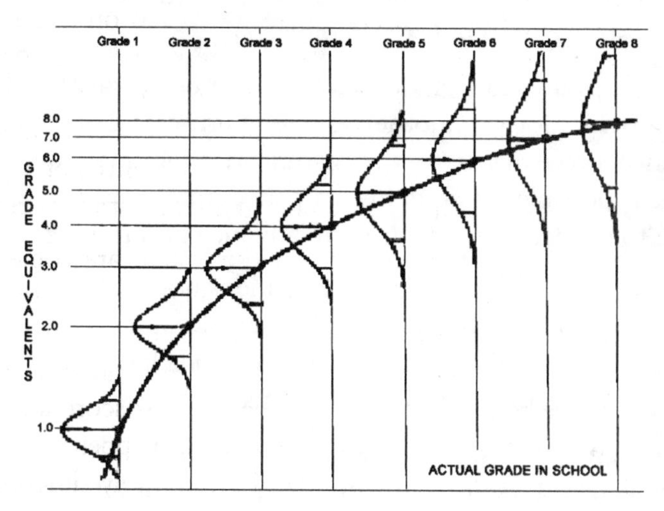

Fig. 2

Note that normal expected reading growth between grades decreases over time, and varies increasingly with student age (notice how the distributions flatten out, or widen, over time—a powerful illustration of the range of individual differences). Expected normal growth also varies depending on where an individual child's level falls on the distribution (higher and lower levels), so it is an error to assume that students who do not improve one GE per year are not experiencing normal gains.

As such, GE scores are best interpreted solely as an indication that a student's performance was above or below average, and not as a reliable measure of student progress. Using GEs to think about relative differences between a specific child and an "average" measure leads to serious errors. For example, it is completely inaccurate to assume that a seventh-grade child who received a GE of 5.1 is reading two years behind grade level, but this is a very common mistake.

If a seventh grader scores a 5.1 GE on a reading test, that does not mean that beginning fifth-grade students got the same score on the same test, or that the child is incapable of doing seventh-grade work. The 5.1 score only means that the student received a score that would be comparable with the average student after the first month of the fifth grade if they were to have taken the same test.

Scores for students not falling exactly on the median point are estimated using an interpolation process which assumes constant growth throughout the year (a source of considerable error). Scores falling outside the range of grades represented on the test are extrapolated—another source of significant error. In other words, GE scores for the students closest to the tails of the distributions are least credible.

Scores for high and low grades also have to be extrapolated. This phenomenon provides for yet another source of error, and also tends to make grade equivalents exaggerate the significance of small differences. For instance, it is possible for students only moderately above the median for their grade to appear as a year or more advanced on the GE scale.

Importantly, the GE scale is not linear, and is not made up of equal intervals, so like percentile rank measures, GE scores cannot be averaged. Every grade equivalent scale is unique to its test, so grade level measures from one test to the next cannot be directly compared.

For all of these reasons, which tend to result in the misuse of test scores, grade equivalent scores are easily and frequently misinterpreted. As such, the International Reading Association has strongly opposed the use of GE measures (Zakaluk and Samuels, 1988).

The Benefits of Lexiles

The Lexile Framework® for Reading was developed over a ten-year period beginning in 1984. The research, sponsored through a series of grants from the National Institute of Child Health and Human Development, was based on the belief that reading scores from an absolute scale would be a meaningful and useful addition to the kinds of norm-referenced data provided by traditional reading comprehension tests, which compare students in relative terms.

The benefits of Lexiles over previous methods of matching students with text have been compelling enough that major book publishers, developers of widely-used reading tests, and a growing number of states and school districts have adopted the Lexile Framework. The U.S. Department of Education has endorsed the use of Lexiles for its America Reads program, and nationally states and districts representing more than 10 million students are now using The Lexile Framework. The use of The Lexile Framework is growing because of the many benefits it offers educators and their students:

- By introducing a single, common scale that can be used to refer both to student ability and test readability, the Lexile Framework does away with the apples-to-oranges method of using incompatible grade levels from standardized test conversions and readability formulas.
- The precision and clarity of the Lexile scale makes it both easy to understand and universally applicable to any test or reading assessment. In effect, the Lexile scale becomes a common language that researchers, educators, students, parents, and the community at large can use to discuss reading challenge.
- Because a wide variety of observations—standardized tests, reading inventories, teacher observations—can be placed on the scale, the Lexile Framework permits us to consider multiple indicators as we judge a student's reading ability and development. This multiple indicator model of assessment lets us determine student ability more accurately and richly than we could from a once-a-year test score (Stenner, 1992, 1996; Stenner, Smith, and Burdick, 1987).

Conclusion

Despite the clear importance of accurately matching students with reading materials that present an appropriate degree of challenge, teachers have had few tools to help them target student reading choices that provided any more accuracy than gut instinct. In the next chapter, we will examine the Lexile Framework, and learn why it presents a usable alternative to traditional text matching techniques.

References

Cook, D. (1986). *A guide to curriculum planning in reading.* Madison, WI: Wisconsin Department of Public Instruction.

Jorgenson, G. (1977). Relationship of classroom behavior to the match between material difficulty and student ability. *Journal of Education Psychology*, 69, 24-32.

Klare, G. (1974). Assessing readability. *Reading Research Quarterly*, 1, 63-102.

Stenner, A.J., Smith, M., & Burdick, D.S. (1987). *Fit of the Lexile Theory to item difficulties on fourteen standardized reading comprehension tests.* Durham, NC: MetaMetrics, Inc.

Stenner, A.J. (1992, April). *Meaning and method in reading comprehension.* Paper presented at the annual meeting of the American Educational Research Association, Division D. Rasch Special Interest Group, San Francisco, CA.

Stenner, A.J. (1996, February). *Measuring reading comprehension with the Lexile Framework.* Paper presented at the Fourth North American Conference on Adolescent/Adult Literacy, Washington, D.C.

Vygotsky, L. (1978). *Mind in society: The development of higher psychological processes.* Cambridge, MA: Harvard University Press.

Zakaluk B., & Samuels, J. (Eds.). (1988). *Readability: Its past, present, and future.* Newark, DE: International Reading Association.

CHAPTER 3

THE LEXILE FRAMEWORK—A COMMON METRIC

Introduction

By introducing a scale that can accurately measure both student ability and text difficulty, the Lexile Framework provides a unique tool for matching students with texts. In this chapter, you will learn what Lexiles are and what they measure, as well as the basic methods for using the Lexile Framework to guide students to appropriate reading experiences.

What are Lexiles?

The word Lexile contains the root "lex", which refers to words, and echoes the word "percentile," a comparative unit of measure. A Lexile is a unit for measuring text difficulty. By determining the level of text difficulty students can comprehend, Lexiles can also be used to determine student reading ability. The two can then be put on the same scale, greatly enhancing the accuracy and utility of comparing students with books. The Lexile Framework is not an instructional system; it is a system of measurement, a framework that calibrates the difficulty of almost any textual material, and determines which students will be able to negotiate that material, quickly and with a high degree of accuracy.

The Lexile Framework is based on a formula that considers two basic variables: the semantic difficulty and the syntactic complexity of the text.

Semantic Difficulty

For the developing reader, new words are difficult when first encountered in print. But as the reader encounters the same word again and again, that word becomes more familiar. Early reading researchers determined that the difficulty of words is a continuum based on exposure, with frequently-encountered words being the easiest and rare words the most difficult (Gray & Leary, 1935). Therefore, knowing the frequency of words as they are used in written and oral communication provides the best means of inferring whether a word will become a part of an individual's vocabulary.

In the Lexile formula, the word frequency measure used was initially drawn from the raw count of how often a given word appeared in a corpus of more than five million words sampled from a broad range of school materials; today, that corpus has been expanded to include more than two hundred million words. Through exploratory data analysis, researchers tested and validated the predictive power of word frequency (Stenner, Smith, & Burdick, 1983).

Syntactic Complexity

Reading researchers have found that the best predictor of the difficulty of a sentence is its length (Davidson, Wilson, & Herman, 1986). Long sentences are likely to contain more clauses, and therefore to communicate not only more information and ideas but an interrelationship between them as well. They also speculate that longer sentences require the reader to retain more in short-term memory in order to negotiate meaning.

The Lexile Map

By analyzing text with a formula that takes both word frequency and sentence length into account, the Lexile Formula assigns a Lexile measure to text. The Lexile measure can be identified by the letter L at its end: 1000L, or 200L, for instance.

The Lexile Map contains an extensive list of criterion texts, from novels and nonfiction books to newspapers and magazines, at various levels on the Lexile scale. The map is available as an annotated, poster-sized graphic. The map makes it easy to "see" how reading develops and to help guide students to select reading materials as they progress.

As we will discuss, by determining student comprehension using the materials on the Lexile Map, it is also possible to assign students a Lexile measure. By allowing you to put readers and texts on the same scale, Lexiles permit you to help students make consistent and highly accurate book selection judgments. It assures that every student will be able to select books that are not too difficult to read, paving the way for many successful individualized reading experiences.

Matching Students with Texts: Basic Methods

The basic method for using the Lexile Framework is to determine a basic Lexile measure for the student and compare it with the Lexile measure of the reading material you are considering for selection. Once you have completed this basic comparison, it is possible to adjust the difficulty of the reading material, taking other factors of the reader, text, and context into account.

Assigning a Lexile Measure

The student Lexile measure marks the level of text a student can read with 75 percent comprehension. In other words, if a student with a Lexile measure of 1000L reads a text with a Lexile number of 1000L, the student should comprehend approximately three quarters of the material. This 75-percent rule corresponds with the student's instructional reading level—the level at which the student can successfully negotiate the material with the use of context clues and other comprehension strategies to fill in the gaps.

The student's Lexile measure establishes a range of readability levels on the Lexile Map, a range that extends about 50L above and 100L below the student measure on the Lexile scale. Taking our 1000L student as an example, this student would have a reading range of between 900L and 1050L on the Lexile Map. If the student attempts material above 1050L, the level of challenge is likely to be too great for the student to be able to construct very much meaning from the text. Likewise, material below 900L will provide that student with little comprehension challenge. Teachers can guide students to reading materials within this range, adjusting difficulty to compensate for the challenges or opportunities the particular reading opportunity provides.

Determining Lexile Measures for Individual Students

A simple procedure for finding an appropriate basic reading range for a student, then, is to present the student with a selection of text from one of the criterion texts on the Lexile Map.

Have the student read the passage aloud, keeping careful note of the miscues the student makes. If necessary, a few questions can be administered to determine the student's comprehension of specific words and passages. If the student appears to be able to read and comprehend at least 75 percent of the passage, you are likely to have established that student's Lexile measure. If the student negotiates the passage with ease, you may repeat the procedure with a passage from a criterion text higher on the Lexile scale; if the student makes numerous miscues, then a lower level text is called for.

Remember that this 75 percent level establishes a high target point of the student's reading range; appropriate text selections are likely to be within a range of 50L above and 100L below the student's Lexile measure.

For example, let's assume you are working with Tom, a second-grader. You might begin by selecting a book typically within range for a student at the beginning of second grade—perhaps a selection like Arnold Lobel's *Days with Frog and Toad* with a Lexile measure of 320L. You have Tom read a passage of the text aloud. Tom reads the passage with only occasional difficulty, struggling with a few words. Based on this observation, you could recommend that Tom try books within the range of 300L to 400L—recommending the lower part of the range for independent book reading, and perhaps using the mid- to upper part of the range to determine Tom's placement for a group reading program.

If Tom had more difficulty reading the passage, so that he often could not get through a sentence without prompting, you would likely have him try again, perhaps with a book at about 250L—perhaps Marcia Vaughan's *Goldsworthy and Mort Blast Off*. On the other hand, if Tom had read the 320L passage with no noticeable difficulty at all, you might try again with a more challenging book at about 400L, H.A. Rey's *Curious George*, for example. Because you are establishing a range of reading materials, it is unnecessary to be absolutely precise. In any event, you will want to repeat the evaluation from time to time to verify your initial observations about Tom and to check on his progress.

Using Lexiles with Formative Assessments

Student Lexile measures can be obtained using a growing number of formative assessment tools, i.e., assessments designed to monitor student progress during instruction (Gronlund, 1977). One example is the Scholastic Reading Inventory or SRI (Scholastic, Inc., 1999), a standardized assessment designed to measure how well students read literature and expository texts of varying difficulties. SRI began as a targeted-level pencil-and-paper test, but is now available in a computer-adaptive test format. Each item consists of a passage that is response-illustrated (a statement is added at the end of the passage with a missing word or phrase followed by four options). The advantage of the SRI for book matching purposes is that the scores are reported in Lexiles. At this writing, Virtual Learning Technologies and the Northwest Evaluation Association were also scheduled to release formative assessments that would report Lexile measures for students.

Using Lexiles with Summative Tests

Summative assessments are achievement tests given at the end of a period of instruction for the purpose of certifying mastery or assigning grades (Gronlund, 1977). Because the Lexile Framework is an absolute, equal-interval scale, standardized reading tests can be directly linked to the Lexile scale by a two-stage process. This process begins by analyzing the test items contained on the test and then administering the test and a Lexile test to a group of students. The result of this process is a correspondence table between the scores on the test and Lexile measures. Lexile measures can then be reported as auxiliary scores on individual student test reports (Petersen, Kolen, and Hoover, 1989).

At this time, the following tests are linked to the Lexile scale: the North Carolina End-of-Grade Test developed by the North Carolina Department of Public Instruction; the Stanford Achievement Series, Ninth Edition (SAT9) and the Stanford Diagnostic Reading Test, Fourth Edition (SDRT4) by Harcourt Educational Measurement; and the Scholastic Reading Inventory by Scholastic Inc. For further information on these tests and other linked tests, refer to the MetaMetrics, Inc. website (www.lexile.com).

Grading Texts

Thousands of commonly-used texts have been analyzed and assigned Lexile measures. We have included a list of familiar books along with their Lexile measures as an appendix to this book. The Lexile Library Database, accessible on the MetaMetrics, Inc. web site (www.lexile.com), contains information on literature, basal readers, textbooks, and even periodicals and newspapers, and includes a search engine that permits you to search for texts in a variety of ways.

A growing number of publishers provide the Lexile measures of books and other materials in their catalogs. Ask your book distributors if they provide Lexile measures for their material.

Targeting Readers with Lexiles

With the basic problem of determining student reading level and text difficulty solved, the teacher now has a tool for student reading levels based on all three sources of reading challenge: the Reader, the Text, and the Context. In Chapter 5, we will discuss in some detail a variety of techniques for using the Lexile Framework to determine appropriate reading materials for a variety of individual and group assignments. For now, we want to suggest the many kinds of uses teachers will find for Lexiles as they attempt to guide students to the right level of reading challenge.

Lexiles Describe a Reading Range

As we have discussed, a student's Lexile measure is a benchmark which we can think of as the high end of that student's reading range, from books that pose little readability challenge to those which require scaffolding for the student to comprehend fully. Targeting the reader requires that we understand this range and what it tells us about what students can achieve under different circumstances.

Suppose, for example, that you wish to have Sam read a book on his own this week. Sam is in the sixth grade and his Lexile measure was 900L on the Scholastic Reading Inventory that he took about a month ago.

A book like *Tom Swift in the Land of Wonders* (900L) is at the high end of Sam's instructional range, because 900L is the point where Sam's predicted comprehension is 75 percent. Sam's independent reading level, however, is at least and probably more than 100 Lexiles below his Lexile measure. So we can quickly calculate that Sam's independent reading range—the range where he is likely to be comfortable when reading books on his own—is between 800L and 900L.

If Sam is interested in reading a book that is at a higher or lower level, or in reading a book without a Lexile measure, you should encourage him to do so. At the same time you should monitor his interest and success in understanding what he is reading, as the Lexile measure is an indication of the fact that a book above 950L may present comprehension problems, and one much below 800L may be too easy to engage him.

Adjusting for the Reader

Of course, the initial adjustment will be for the basic developmental reading level of the student.

The Lexile Map and Lexile reading ranges give teachers a quick and accurate way to determine which texts are likely to be within a student's basic range of comprehension.

Beyond this basic determination, it is possible to adjust for the interests, experience, and background of the student. A student who needs to compensate for a lack of prior literacy experiences is likely to find any text challenging beyond its basic difficulty: Teachers can use Lexiles to guide such a student to texts at the lower end of the student's Lexile range. Similarly, advanced students can be adequately challenged to promote reading development by guiding them to texts at the midpoint of their Lexile range, or slightly above. Challenging new topics or genres may be approached in the same manner.

Another reader-focused adjustment relates to the student's motivation and purpose. If a student is highly-motivated for a particular reading task—say, for instance, self-selected free reading—the teacher may confidently suggest books higher in his or her Lexile range (or possibly above). If the student is less motivated, or perhaps even somewhat intimidated, by a reading task, material at the lower end of his or her Lexile range (or even below) can provide the basic comprehension support to keep the student from feeling overwhelmed.

Various tools are available to help teachers monitor these reader-centered concerns. Interest inventories can help pinpoint topics that will prove especially motivational. Reading logs and reading portfolios, especially those used to track self-selected reading, can provide valuable clues as to the student's areas of comfort and challenge. And, as always, there is no substitute for the careful and compassionate observation of an experienced educator. Information gained from all of these sources can help teachers adjust text suggestions to the appropriate level in the student's Lexile range for any particular assignment.

Adjusting for the Text

The genre and format of specific texts can provide a varying level of challenge to students beyond the readability of the text. Experienced primary reading teachers are especially aware of these issues: the student who is afraid to move beyond picture books, even though his reading comprehension skills are up to the task; the challenges posed by the introduction of chapter books and nonfiction works. Even type size and use of color can be cues that influence the student's expectations of the level of challenge a text poses. For more developed readers, new genres of material or the requirement to search out specific facts from text present additional challenges.

The Lexile Framework provides teachers a way to use their awareness of these challenges to adjust the difficulty of assigned texts. When students confront new kinds of texts, the introduction can be softened and made less intimidating by guiding the student to easier reading. On the other hand, students who are comfortable with a particular genre or format can be challenged to concentrate at readability levels which will prevent boredom and promote the greatest rate of development of vocabulary and comprehension skills.

Adjusting for Context

Similarly, the Lexile Framework can be used to adjust difficulty levels for challenges provided by environmental pressures, as well as the goals and expectations of the reading experience. Perhaps the most common adjustment will be for the varying expectations of free, storybook reading versus reading done for study or research purposes. Reading required for a major assignment or to pass an important exam can also be adjusted for.

Of course, teachers do not always have the luxury of adjusting texts for individual readers; all students will be expected to work from the same textbook, for instance, and the teacher may not have the means to find or create a range of differently-leveled materials to meet the widely-ranging needs of his or her class. However, awareness of how the difficulty of the material compares with the competence of the students will allow teachers to compensate when required materials are either too difficult or too easy, either for an individual or for larger numbers of students within the class. In Chapters 5 and 6 we will discuss a variety of methods for supporting materials which are not within the student's Lexile range.

Perhaps the most important way that Lexiles enhance the educational environment is by giving teachers, students, parents, and others a common way to understand reading ability and text difficulty. A student's Lexile range can be communicated without the stigma often attached to grade-level assessments. Teachers and students can set goals for reading achievement using numbers that apply equally well to the student and the text. And parents can receive reading lists and other support materials that help them encourage their children's development.

Conclusion

By providing a common metric that can be applied to both text difficulty and student comprehension skill, one that has more precision and less potential stigma than grade equivalent leveling, the Lexile Framework offers educators a flexible and easy-to-use tool to help target students with texts that present the appropriate degree of reading challenge. When you know the Lexile measure of the book and the approximate Lexile measure for the student, you can determine accurately whether the student should be able to read and comprehend that text. This enhanced targeting makes reading more successful for students, increasing both their ability to learn from text and their reading motivation. In addition, the clarity and flexibility of the Lexile scale makes it an excellent way to communicate about student reading goals and achievements with students, parents, and other educators.

References

Davidson, A., Wilson, P., & Herman, G. (1986). *Effects of syntactic connections and organizing cues on text comprehension.* Champaign, IL: Center for the Study of Reading.

Fielding, L., & Roller, C. (1992). Making difficult books accessible and easy books acceptable. *The Reading Teacher,* 45, 9.

Gray, W., & Leary, B. (1935). *What makes a book readable?* Chicago: University of Chicago Press.

Gronlund, N. (1977). *Constructing achievement tests* (2nd ed.). Englewood Cliffs, NJ: Prentice-Hall.

Monson, D., & Sebesta, S. (1991). Reading preferences. In J. Flood, J. Jensen, D. Lapp, & J. Squire (Eds.). *Handbook of research on teaching the English language arts.* New York: Macmillan Publishing Company.

Morrow, L. (1991). Promoting Voluntary Reading. In J. Flood, J. Jensen, D. Lapp, & J. Squire (Eds.), *Handbook of research on teaching the English language arts.* New York: Macmillan Publishing Company.

Mosenthal, P. (1999). Understanding engagement: Historical and political contexts. In J. Guthrie & D. Alverman (Eds.), *Engaged reading: Processes, practices and policy implications.* New York: Teachers College Press.

Petersen, N.S., Kolen, M.J., & Hoover, H.D. (1989). Scaling, norming, and equating. In R.L. Linn (Ed.), *Educational Measurement* (3rd ed., pp. 221-262). New York: American Council on Education and Macmillan Publishing Company.

Scholastic, Inc. (1999). *Scholastic Reading Inventory—Technical Manual #1.* New York: Author.

Stenner, A. J. (1999). *Matching students to text: The targeted reader.* New York: Scholastic Center for Literacy & Learning.

Stenner, A. J. (1997). *The LexileFramework: A map to higher levels of achievement.* Durham, NC: MetaMetrics, Inc.

Stenner, A.J. (1996, February). *Measuring reading comprehension with the Lexile Framework.* Paper presented at the Fourth North American Conference on Adolescent/Adult Literacy, Washington, D.C.

Stenner, A.J., & Burdick, D.S. (1997). *The objective measurement of reading comprehension: In response to technical questions raised by the California Department of Education Technical Study Group.* Durham, NC: MetaMetrics, Inc.

Stenner, A.J., Smith, M., & Burdick, D. (1983). Toward a theory of construct definition. *Journal of Educational Measurement,* 20, 305-315.

CHAPTER 4

WHY LEXILES WORK

Introduction

For years, reading experts have been aware of the need for better ways to perform the critical task of matching students with texts. In the late 1970s, A.J. Stenner and Malbert Smith began working on new ways of measuring student ability and text difficulty. With a series of grants from the National Institute of Child Health and Human Development, the two led a team of researchers in the development of a single metric that could be applied to both text and reader. The result of more than a decade of research and testing of this concept is *The Lexile Framework® for Reading.*

An Absolute Scale for Reading

A scale is absolute if any example of the entity to be measured can be placed on the scale, regardless of the instruments and conditions of measurement. For a scale of reading ability, a scale is absolute if any student can be placed on the scale, regardless of the kind of test used or how other students performed on the test. As we discussed in Chapter 2, most standardized reading tests are relative; the scores they provide tell you only how the student performed compared to other students who took the same test. For this reason, you cannot compare a student's percentile score on one reading test with scores on another without performing a variety of statistical calculations. As an absolute scale of reading ability, the Lexile Framework provides a tool for measuring and tracking student reading skills that can be compared between students and between different assessment techniques. In addition, it can be used to track the development of a student's ability.

Another useful aspect of the Lexile Framework is that it consists of regular intervals. Each Lexile unit is a standard measurement of text difficulty and/or student reading competence. In contrast, the percentile scores provided by reading tests are based on the familiar bell-shaped distribution curve, with most students centered around the mean score and decreasing numbers toward either end. Because of this distribution, the difference in ability between a student scoring at the 80th percentile on a test and a student scoring at the 90th percentile is not the same as the difference between students scoring at the 50th and 60th percentiles—even though it appears to be the same ten-unit difference in each case. As a standard unit of reading ability, the Lexile is easy to understand and apply in a variety of situations.

We can make a useful analogy if we think about thermometers. The Celsius and Fahrenheit scales on a thermometer are examples of absolute scales. Therefore, if we know that it is 55 degrees Fahrenheit in Chicago and 75 degrees Fahrenheit in Miami, we know that it is 20 degrees cooler in Chicago than it is in Miami. Or, if it happens to be January, we might say that the 55-degree-day in Chicago is the warmest January day in Chicago's history. It does not matter which thermometers are used in either city, when the measurements are taken, or what the temperature might be anywhere else in the world. And even though the Celsius and Fahrenheit scales measure temperature differently, because they are both absolute scales we can convert measurements taken in one scale to the other with a simple formula.

Imagine if all the thermometers in the world had to be recalibrated every day so the scale would always reflect the average of temperatures everywhere in the world! Now imagine that, instead of the standard mercury thermometer, there were many kinds of thermometers, each using different ways to measure temperature. You could not know what 55 degrees meant without knowing what kind of thermometer was used and what temperature all the other thermometers of that kind read on that day. You would have to be a trained statistician to make sense of the simplest weather report!

While reading tests that measure a student's abilities relative to other students have important uses, our thermometer analogy helps us understand why they can be so difficult to use in determining the appropriate level of text difficulty for a given student. By providing an absolute scale with regular intervals, the Lexile Framework provides teachers with a tool that is as useful for measuring student ability as a thermometer is for measuring temperature.

Measurement Error in Assessment

As with all standardized test instruments, formal reading assessments are based on a true score theorem, which states simply that the score that an individual gets on a test represents a combination of the individual's true ability and some degree of measurement error. What could cause this error?

It could be any number of factors, from differences in testing procedures, a testing bias, or simply the mood and physical well being of the test-taker on a given day.

Every test score is presumed to contain random error caused by factors (such as mood) that are different for each individual test-taker. In addition, certain kinds of systematic errors (i.e., ones that would affect the scores of all test-takers) exist and can be corrected by performing a statistical analysis of the results. While it is possible to estimate the reliability of a test score, we simply cannot know for sure what the difference is between the test-taker's true score on the test and his or her true ability.

It is possible to estimate the extent of the difference between a student's true ability and his observed score. When this is done the result is an estimate of the error associated with each score on the test (standard error of measurement), not just an overall estimate for the test. The standard error of measurement can identify a range in which a test-taker's true score is likely located, but it cannot pinpoint the true score. When a student takes an assessment that is targeted to his reading level (i.e., the middle range of the test's reportable scores is consistent with his reading level), then the standard error of measurement is minimized. When a student takes an assessment that is not well targeted, then there is more uncertainty that the observed score accurately represents the student's true ability.

One way to minimize measurement error is to collect multiple observations of the individual's ability; by comparing the results, you would then be able to narrow the margin of error and have a more accurate idea of the test-taker's true score (Trochim, 1999). As we've discussed, however, without a common, absolute metric to place these test scores on, comparing one standardized test score to another is precisely what we cannot do.

A single student test score reported in Lexiles is susceptible to measurement error just as any other kind of test score. It too is an approximation of a student's true measure on a given day.

What the Lexile Framework allows us to do, however, is to place not one but several measures on the same Lexile scale, and to compare them with other information. By allowing the use of uniform multiple indicators, Lexiles provide us with a way to minimize measurement error and arrive at a more precise picture of a student's true ability.

How the Lexile Framework Measures Text Difficulty

All symbol systems, such as mathematics, music, and language have both semantic and syntactic components. In math, for instance, the semantic units are numbers and operators, which are combined to make equations based on the syntactic rules of math (so we write 2+2=4, not =2 2 4 +). In music, the semantic unit is the note, arranged according to musical syntax into chords and phrases. In language, the semantic units are words that vary in familiarity, and the syntactic structures are sentences, which vary in complexity.

Semantic Difficulty

Most operationalizations of semantic difficulty are proxies for the probability that an individual will encounter a word in familiar text and thus be able to infer its meaning (Bormouth, 1966). Based on frequency studies of more than five million words sampled from a broad range of school materials, Carroll, Davies, and Richman (1971) observed that knowing the frequency of words as they are used in written and oral communication provided the best means of inferring the likelihood that a word would be encountered by a reader and thus become a part of that individual's receptive vocabulary.

Using two forms of the Peabody Picture Vocabulary Test, MetaMetrics, Inc. researchers analyzed more than 50 semantic variables to determine which were the most valid indicators of text difficulty (Stenner, Smith, and Burdick, 1983). These variables included part of speech, number of letters, number of syllables, the modal grade at which the word appeared in school materials, content classification, and word frequency, as well as various algebraic transformations of these variables. The mean log word frequency had the highest correlation with text difficulty ($r = -0.779$) for the items on the two forms of the test. This is the measurement used to determine the semantic difficulty of text in the Lexile system.

It should be noted that word frequency is not the number of times a specific word appears in a specific passage. It is the frequency of the word in the corpus that is employed by the Lexile Analyzer®. At the current time, a corpus of over 200 million words is used when analyzing text.

Syntactic Complexity

Sentence length is a powerful indicator of the syntactic complexity of a passage. Having more words alone does not make a sentence more difficult, but longer sentences do tend to contain more clauses, and therefore convey more information as well as the relationship between the pieces of information the sentence contains. Klare (1963) speculated that the syntactic complexity of sentences depends on how much of a load they place on short-term memory: The more information bits and relationships you have to keep in mind to get at the meaning of the sentence, the more syntactically complex that sentence is. Again using the Peabody Individual Achievement Test, MetaMetrics, Inc. researchers found that the log of the mean sentence length was the best predictor of passage difficulty (Stenner, 1996).

The Lexile Framework, then, works by combining measurements of word frequency and sentence length for any passage into an algebraic equation that determines both the semantic and syntactic difficulty of that passage. This equation can then be used to scale the difficulty of English language text; it can also be used to place reading comprehension test items on the same scale, so that reading test scores can be reportable in Lexiles.

Calibrating the Scale

Once the word-frequency and sentence-length measurements were combined to produce a regression equation that could explain the variance in reading comprehension task difficulties, the regression needed to be calibrated to provide the standard unit of measurement—the Lexile (Stenner, Smith, Horiban, & Smith, 1987a). This calibration was determined using base texts as "anchor points." In developing the Lexile scale, the Rasch item response theory model was used to estimate difficulties of items and abilities of persons on the logit scale (Rasch, 1980; Wright & Stone, 1979).

In a measurement system, anchor points help determine the scale of measurement. For most thermometers, for instance, the anchor points are the boiling and freezing points of water. For the Lexile scale, the anchor points are text from seven basal primers for the low end, and text from the Grolier Electronic Encyclopedia for the high end. These points correspond to text typically used in the middle of first grade, to average text encountered by adults in the workplace. A Lexile, then, represents 1/1000th of the difference between the comprehensibility of the primers and the comprehensibility of the encyclopedia. The low-end anchor on the Lexile scale was assigned a value of 200 to reduce the occurrence of negative Lexile values in very simple text (Stenner, 1996).

Validating the Framework

Finally, to validate the Lexile Framework, researchers used the Lexile formula to analyze 1,780 reading comprehension test items appearing on nine nationally-normed tests (Stenner, Smith, Horiban, & Smith, 1987a). The study correlated the difficulties of the test items with the Lexile calibrations produced by a computer analyzing the text of the items using the Lexile equation. While they learned that certain types of text—poetry, lists, and other kinds of noncontinuous material—did not fit with the Lexile Framework, the equation did correlate with the measurement of reading comprehension used on the tests, no matter what kind of test item, skill objective, or response mode was used in the tests. Additional analyses verified these findings with leveled material in basal readers (Stenner, Smith, Horiban, & Smith, 1987b).

The result of this decade-long research is a tool that provides a standard measurement that can be used to make useful comparative judgments about student reading comprehension and text difficulty, as well as to match students with texts based on their ability and needs. As we have discussed, this kind of match is a powerful tool for helping students feel that their reading ability is appropriately challenged by the text at hand; this in turn creates the conditions under which reading can become an optimal "flow" experience for students, helping them build vocabulary, comprehension, and higher-order thinking skills while increasing their sense of mastery and their intrinsic motivation for reading.

Conclusion

Standing behind the increased accuracy and usefulness of the Lexile Framework is a scientific approach to understanding reading challenge, validated by more than a decade of research, design, and testing. Our discussion in this chapter can only serve to introduce the reader to the psychometric elements that are built into the Lexile scale. Even a cursory understanding of these issues is important to classroom teachers, however, because it aids in the understanding of what readability formulas and reading assessments can and cannot do—an understanding that is essential for their proper use.

As with any such formula, a Lexile measurement has limitations. While it is a highly sophisticated estimate of reading difficulty or ability, it is still only an estimate, and there are many things it cannot take into account—the past experiences and background knowledge of the reader, the unique challenges presented by reading context and reading purpose. Rather than a panacea, the Lexile Framework provides teachers with a unique tool to augment their other assessments and observations as they make individual judgments on the proper reading intervention for any given student. We believe—and our experience with teachers using the Lexile Framework today has shown—that it is a tool teachers will value highly.

References

Bormouth, J.R. (1966). Readability: New approach. *Reading Research Quarterly*, 7, 79-132.

Carroll, J.B., Davies, P., & Richman, R. (1971). *The word frequency book*. Boston: Houghton Mifflin.

Klare, G.R. (1963). *The measurement of readability*. Ames, IA: Iowa State University Press.

Rasch, G.A. (1980). *Probablistic models for some intelligence and attainment tests.* Chicago: The University of Chicago Press (first published in 1960).

Stenner, A.J. (1996, February). *Measuring reading comprehension with the Lexile Framework.* Paper presented at the Fourth North American Conference on Adolescent/Adult Literacy, Washington, D.C.

Stenner, A.J., Smith, M. & Burdick, D.S. (1983). Toward a theory of construct definition. *Journal of Education Measurement,* 20(4), 305-315.

Stenner, A. J., Smith, D.R., Horabin, I., & Smith, M. (1987a). *Fit of the Lexile Theory to item difficulties of fourteen standardized reading comprehension tests*. Durham, NC: MetaMetrics, Inc.

Stenner, A. J., Smith, D.R., Horabin, I., & Smith, M. (1987b). *Fit of the Lexile Theory to sequenced units from eleven basal series.* Durham, NC: MetaMetrics, Inc.

Trochim, W. (1999). *The research methods knowledge base* (2nd ed.). Ithaca, New York: Cornell Custom Publishing, Cornell University.

Wright, B.D., & Stone, M. H. (1979). *Best test design.* Chicago: MESA Press.

CHAPTER 5

READER, TEXT, CONTEXT: USING LEXILES IN COMMON READING SITUATIONS

Introduction

As we described in Chapter 3, the Lexile Framework provides a scale that can help teachers moderate the difficulty of recommended or assigned texts by balancing the difficulty/competence factors presented by the Reader, Text, and Context (Chapter 2). While we will discuss a number of specific suggestions for making those moderations, the basic rule of thumb is quite simple.

- The student's Lexile measure represents the level at which the student can read with 75 percent comprehension. This measure defines a range of reading levels that extend about 100 below and 50 Lexiles above the student's Lexile measure. Reading above this range presents a level of difficulty that prevents students from inferring meaning from the text; texts below this range do not present significant challenge to the student and may lead to boredom and disengagement.

- Overall, you should use text lower in the student's Lexile range when factors make that reading situation more challenging, threatening, or unfamiliar. Use texts at or above the student's Lexile measure to stimulate challenge and growth, or when you will be adding additional support such as background teaching or discussion.

- For unsupported independent reading, avoid texts that are above the top end of the student's Lexile range whenever possible (although, as we'll discuss later, such texts may be used with additional instructional support by the teacher).

- In all reading situations, use the Lexile scale as an accurate and easy way to communicate with students, parents, and other educators about student abilities, text difficulties, and goals for reading comprehension growth and achievement.

As you begin to work with the Lexile Framework, you will gradually gain confidence in your ability to use the Lexile scale to make appropriate adjustments in text difficulty for different students and different situations. The following are general recommendations that will introduce you to the process.

Adjusting for the Stages of Reading Development

While we sometimes think of reading development as a steady progression of new vocabulary and comprehension strategies, in fact the process of reading changes markedly as readers mature. As the eminent reading researcher, Dr. Jeanne Chall (1996), wrote, "The reading of the stumbling beginner is not the reading of the fluent third grader nor of the skilled college freshman. It takes most people about twenty years to reach the highest stage of reading development. Some people reach it much faster, others take longer, and still others may not reach it at all" (p. 7).

Seventy-five years ago, William Gray (1925) reported that "a careful study of the progress of children in reading shows that they pass through different stages of development in acquiring mature (reading) habits" (p. 21). He determined that there were five stages of reading development from kindergarten to adulthood. Since Gray's initial work, there have been other complementary reading stage theories advanced, all describing in practical terms the developing cognitive and linguistic abilities of the growing child who learns to read.

The most compelling refinement of this idea was advanced in 1983 by Chall, who spent a major portion of her career studying and refining reading stages. Chall observed six stages children pass through from early childhood to reading maturity.

Stage 0 is the Pre-reading Stage, from birth to age 6. In this stage children grow in their use of words and syntax of language. They begin to associate words and sounds, identify rhymes and alliteration, and acquire basic phonemic awareness. They begin to understand that words contain parts and that those parts, in turn, can be used to form words.

Stage 1 is the Initial Reading, or Decoding Stage, which typically corresponds to the development of six- and seven-year-olds in first and second grade. This stage is marked by the child's learning to associate arbitrary letters with the corresponding parts of spoken words. In this stage, beginning readers gain knowledge about what it means to read something, what letters are for, and to notice the subtle differences between similar-sounding words. This stage culminates in the child's ability to use her knowledge to decode words she has not seen before in print.

Stage 2 is marked by confirmation, fluency, and "ungluing" from print, a process generally seen in seven- and eight-year-olds in grades two and three. In this stage, readers consolidate what they have learned in Stage 1 by reading familiar books. Rereading encourages fluency as well. Most readers learn to use their decoding skills along with repeated exposures to familiar words to develop competence and confidence, thereby improving fluency and speed. Proper development through this stage requires rereading many easy and familiar texts as a part of reading instruction, as well as functional and recreational reading during other parts of the school day.

Stage 3 is the first step toward reading for learning and exploration. During Stages 1 and 2, readers concentrate on relating print to speech. Beginning with Stage 3, readers are more concerned with relating print to ideas. Chall split this stage in two parts, 3A and 3B. Stage 3A is when students begin primarily reading new information for assigned and self-selected purposes. Readers at this stage of development begin reading to learn and enjoy acquiring conventional knowledge through reading. This stage typically occurs in grades 4 through 6, ages 9 to 11. In Stage 3B, students read to acquire and synthesize information from multiple sources. Readers begin developing their individual reading tastes and preferences. This stage typically spans the middle-school years.

Stage 4 is a stage of reading to learn, to enjoy, and to accomplish academic work—reading to do. During this stage, which is associated with high-school students, readers increase their understanding of complementary and conflicting points of view through reading, critically analyze texts, and further develop their reading interests.

Stage 5 is the most mature level of reading, during which the reader moves from a concrete understanding of text knowledge to a more abstract level of understanding and the awareness that reading involves assessing and evaluating multiple points of view in order to refine one's own view of the world. Readers at this stage, typically college-level and beyond, are motivated by their own purposes and tastes. They increase their efficiency of reading for career purposes as well as the breadth and depth of their reading experiences and tastes.

The successive nature of these reading stages holds several important messages for teachers. First, how students react to reading changes as they develop. At different stages, readers are cognitively engaged in doing different things with print; eye movements, reading rates, attention to the decoding process, fluency, and focus on meaning all change throughout the reader's development. Secondly, the reader's vocabulary and comprehension strategies become richer and more complex as the content of the texts they encounter becomes richer and more challenging. As content complexity grows, either the child needs to have a broader and deeper expanse of prior knowledge and background, or the teacher must supply the background information before reading can be successful. Finally, at any given stage a child may persist in certain cognitive and language habits that end up delaying a transition to the next stage—the reader is, in Chall's phrase, "glued" to those habits.

Stage 0: Pre-reading

Stage 1: Initial reading or decoding

Stage 2: Confirmation and fluency

Stage 3: Reading for learning and exploration

Stage 4: Reading to learn, enjoy, and accomplish academic work

Stage 5: Mature reading

Using Lexiles to Adjust for Stages 1 and 2

Readers who have not yet acquired the ability to recognize and decode unknown words need to practice their reading with materials that control the vocabulary levels enough so that they can understand what they are reading as they practice. There are two primary ways to accomplish this: 1) adjust the Lexile levels of recommended reading materials in a more controlled way; and 2) select the materials in a more controlled way, to compensate for the less mature reader's cognitive demands.

Stage 1 and Stage 2 readers are not yet skilled at deciphering words from context; furthermore, they are not proficient with decoding the most basic 5,000 to 6,000 words in their own listening vocabularies. These limitations hamper their reading fluency and speed, making it more difficult for them to infer meaning from text. Because of the cognitive demands of word recognition as they read, these readers need more practice with print materials that contain close to 95 percent of the words they know on sight, considerably more than older, more mature readers need.

Younger and less mature readers are more apt to struggle. Their main goal is to achieve a degree of fluency and competence. To enable them to reach their goal, we recommend two primary adjustments: one for recognizable words and one for familiar texts.

Adjustment for recognizable words Until reaching a level of 300L, Stage 1 and Stage 2 students should focus on materials with Lexile measures at about 50L below their own personal Lexile measures for independent reading practice. For shared reading experiences, Stage 1 and Stage 2 students may practice with materials up to their personal Lexile measures. These early readers should only work with materials that are at or above their personal Lexile measures for individual or group reading aloud activities. Shared reading or reading aloud experiences are an important tool for introducing early readers to new and more difficult materials, drawing words from their listening vocabularies and expanding and refining their basic reading vocabularies.

Adjustment for familiar texts Most independent reading activities for early readers involves reading aloud to an interested and supportive adult. With these activities, keeping the Lexile range of the materials at or below the child's Lexile measure is not necessary—primarily because the child is, or should be, rereading materials that are very familiar to him. Rather than stumbling along through unfamiliar text, children need rereading experiences with familiar text to gain confidence as they gain competence. Most of the texts that early readers approach should be attempted not once, but many times, to reinforce existing reading vocabularies and expand them. The best way to foster this is by rereading activities of favorite and familiar materials.

Adjustments for Stages 3 and Beyond

Automaticity A critical rite-of-passage in reading development occurs when the young reader's cognitive load shifts from sounding out and recognizing words to thinking about what the text says, or reading for meaning. If a reader is not yet reading fluently and attending to the meaning of the text, if the reader does not yet have a rapid and accurate facility with word recognition, the reader—regardless of age!—has not yet moved into Stage 3 and is less mature in his reading development. If, however, readers have passed this threshold and are reading with automaticity, they are indeed a different kind of a reader in a more mature state of reading development.

This critical threshold is important not only for elementary level teachers: Middle school and high school teachers need to pay close attention! Readers who have not yet reached automaticity, who have not passed into Stage 3 of reading development, regardless of their age, need to be targeted somewhat differently than more mature readers.

Targeting Older Readers for Independent Reading In our K-12 educational systems, we require readers in Stages 3 and above to read for meaning. Typically we expect readers beginning in grades 3 and thereafter to become "unglued from print," that the reader's attention and cognitive abilities are focused mostly on understanding the text, not sounding out the words. By the time they are in fourth grade, almost all students are expected to acquire much of their content area learning by reading and much of their vocabulary development through context. Chall calls the stage of reading that typically begins at fourth grade "reading for learning the new." From this point on, in school and outside of school, the main purposes of reading are to acquire new information, explore new viewpoints, and develop our understanding of the world.

When we target readers with a range of Lexiled books we need to distinguish between targeting Stage 1 and 2 readers and targeting readers who have passed the threshold to Stages 3 and beyond. For readers in Stages 3 and above, the targeting process for independent reading is relatively easy: The targeted Lexile level for independent reading can be a range of 50 or more Lexiles above and 100 or more Lexiles below the individual student's tested Lexile measure.

As we discussed in Chapter 3, when a reader has the same Lexile measure as a text, the reader should be able to read that text with 75 percent comprehension, thereby "targeting" that reader at a point that corresponds to an instructional reading level.

If you have a Lexile measure of 1000L, for instance, then you should be able to read text that measures 1000L with 75 percent comprehension. When reader and text measures match, the reader is "targeted." Targeted readers report competence, confidence, and control over text. Remember, the level at which a student is being challenged by exposure to new vocabulary and concepts without being frustrated is the point at which the Lexile Framework matches readers to texts. This match between reader and texts is the reading level at which reading practice will promote maximum growth.

Older, more mature readers are by definition also more flexible readers. They have learned to implement many different reading strategies as they progress through the stages of reading development. Even for more mature readers, however, we know that when comprehension levels drop to 50 percent, readers report frustration, inadequacy, and lack of control. Older readers have a certain range of Lexiles that we need to stay within to ensure that they remain engaged and continue to read for meaning. The more mature the reader, the wider the range may be, especially if the content is familiar or interesting to that reader, or that reader has an extensive background with that content.

Always remember that as children move to higher stages of reading development, the content complexity grows. As the complexity grows, the child needs to have a broader and deeper expanse of prior knowledge and background to understand the technical and content-specific vocabulary. If the content is new to the student, either background information must be supplied increasingly by the teacher (for example, pre-teaching vocabulary and concepts), or the Lexile level of the material needs to remain closer to the individual student's Lexile measure. Conversely, with adequate teacher support and discussion, students can utilize materials at a higher Lexile measure than may be appropriate for independent reading. In Chapters 5 and 6, we will discuss methods by which teachers can broaden the range of texts that students can access successfully.

Adjusting for Text Characteristics

The other side of the matching equation is to know the Lexile measures for the texts you want to use. You will find the Lexile measures of many popular texts listed in the appendix to this book. The Lexile Map contains 38 benchmark texts of all kinds from primary to post-high-school levels. In addition, the MetaMetrics, Inc. web site, www.lexile.com, contains The Lexile Library, a database of more than 20,000 texts for which Lexile measures have been determined. The Lexile Library is a collection of literature titles, each of which has been assigned a Lexile measure. The Lexile Library also includes magazines, newspapers, textbooks, and other common text materials. The database contains a search engine which permits you to search for texts by ISBN, title, author, and Lexile range. New materials are being added continually for use by teachers, librarians, parents, and developing readers. With this collection, teachers can recommend specific titles and supplemental texts to individual students.

Adjusting for Format and Genre

As we discussed in Chapter 2, the format and genre of the text itself provide various levels of perceived challenge to the student. In general, we tend to perceive familiar and pleasant tasks as easy; unfamiliar tasks, or tasks which we are performing primarily to meet the expectations of other people, tend to be perceived as more difficult.

Many aspects of a text can be cues that influence a student's expectations about the difficulty of the text at hand: the presence or lack of illustrations; the length of a book or article; the density and type size of the text; the topic, genre, author, and so on. Similarly, students will perceive free reading of self-selected books for pleasure to be less difficult that reading a textbook assignment or doing research for a term paper. It is not enough simply to be aware of a book's readability level; these other text factors must also be taken into account if the student's reading experience is to be a successful one.

In general, "easier" texts (that is, more familiar or self-selected ones) should be read at the student's Lexile measure—the point at which the student must rely on a fair number of context clues and inferences in order to infer meaning from the text. Reading practice at this level will encourage the student to develop a larger and richer vocabulary, a greater arsenal of comprehension skills, and greater ability to think in higher-order ways—while still providing a level of comprehensibility that will avoid student frustration. In short, reading of these "easy" texts at the student's Lexile measure will provide the balance of challenge and success that permits reading to "flow."

When less familiar texts are assigned, teachers must keep in mind that the lack of familiarity and self-direction will provide an increasing sense of challenge. In such instances, either students must be guided to reading at the lower end of their Lexile range, or the teacher must provide additional support to make the reading experience successful for students.

Supporting Tough Texts

Up to now, we have mainly been discussing the use of Lexiles to adjust the text difficulty in relation to the needs of the student. However, teachers will not always have the luxury or desire to adjust the readability levels at which they recommend or assign texts to students. Classes typically must rely on standard textbooks, which students will have to be able to use regardless of their reading level; the same holds true for many other teaching materials as well. This presents relatively little difficulty for students whose Lexile measure is above that of the required material; while it may not be much of a challenge, such students will at least be able to comprehend the meaning of the text. Of greater concern are the many instances in which the comprehension skills of an individual student—or even of an entire class—place a particular required text beyond their Lexile range and, consequently, their ability to learn from it.

Beyond such concerns, we may unnecessarily limit students and narrow their range of reading if we prevent them from exposure to texts that may be beyond their optimal Lexile range. Ninth graders can read and understand even an income tax form when the teacher prepares them for reading it. Fourth graders can read an article from the *Encyclopedia Americana* when the teacher pre-teaches the vocabulary and concepts they need to know in order to comprehend it. The best guideline available for understanding how to target readers in instructional settings is to know the Lexile measure of the material and to supply greater and greater amounts of the vocabulary and concepts contained as the text diverges higher and higher from the students' Lexile measures. With instructional reading, the limit to text difficulty depends upon the intensity of instructional support that the teacher provides before the reading activity takes place.

What does the teacher need to consider when providing instructional support? Manzo (1975) supplies the following six principles for guiding comprehension instruction:

- Use Front-Loading Techniques. Front-loading refers to attempts to empower pupils before they read. Front-loading techniques are used to reduce potential vocabulary obstacles to comprehension, activate relevant prior knowledge, and provide specific information on text structure and actual facts covered in the text. This enables students to engage a reading selection with what amounts to an elevated reading quotient. Front-loading techniques obviously are more important with content-rich material than narrative and are important with young, remedial, or culturally or linguistically different youngsters.

Strategies That Cause Students to Make Transformations

Readers are liable to be more alert, active, and engaged by a requirement to manipulate and transform the text from the author's words into those of the reader. Try to include this "active ingredient" in every teaching episode and with any teaching method you may be using. Reconstructive transformations include tasks such as:

- Translating, or retelling what one has read, with the text available
- Recalling and retelling, without looking back at the text
- Rewriting, or summarizing, with the text available
- Summarizing without consulting the text
- Outlining with and without available text
- Representing the text in a student-constructed graphic overview or illustration, with the text available for reference

Instruction on Authentic Text and Tasks

There are many possible ways to achieve some level of relevance in school. Teaching methods and materials that are selected need to come closer to the ways that real interests are built and language is used and learned. This is best done largely through the careful construction of a conducive environment that can excite interest and has a life-like or problem-based orientation.

- ***Create Instructional Conversations:*** Instructional conversation is known by several other names, such as "responsive teaching," "reciprocity," and "cognitive apprenticeship." By any name, the idea is to create authentic interaction between people, who just happen to be teacher and students, or students with one another. Such interactions tend to rouse minds to life and provide opportunities for effective thinking to be modeled, and for ineffective thinking to be detected and fixed in an "in-line" way while you are teaching.

Strategies, Not Skills

Each lesson should be crafted so that possible strategies can be imparted for students to use in reading and learning situations. Accordingly, it is important to focus on teaching students to use strategies such as self-monitoring and self-fixing, and thus to encourage them to assume increasing responsibility for their own reading and learning needs.

- ***Use Question Types That Match Instructional Objectives:*** Question types typically are categorized according to some perceived organization of the cognitive domain, such as Bloom's Taxonomy and Marzano's Dimensions of Thinking and Dimensions of Learning.

Adjustments for the Reading Context

Reading/Language Arts Program

A growing number of teachers are recognizing the importance of self-selected, literature-based reading in helping students develop not only skills but reading motivation as well. The challenge with such programs in the past is that it has been very difficult for teachers to keep track of each student's changing development and provide the kind of individualized support that helps students achieve the maximum reading gain from free reading.

The Lexile Framework supplies a program of individualized, self-selected reading that permits teachers to set clear achievement goals with students and monitor their progress toward their desired objectives. With the simple, accurate, and nonjudgmental language of the Lexile Framework as an aid, teachers and students can communicate productively about student reading ability and the difficulty posed by various texts.

For example, Lexiles can be used within a contract-style goal setting and monitoring program. At the beginning of each grading period, teachers may have one-on-one meetings with students to review the reading they've done and discuss what kinds of goals they can mutually agree to for the coming period. Using Lexiles minimizes the guesswork and confusion in setting appropriate goals. Teachers can encourage students to concentrate their reading within an appropriate Lexile range, and provide reading lists that guide students to books within that range that meet their interests.

If the situation calls for introducing a student to a new genre or author, the teacher can help ease the potentially intimidating situation by permitting the student choose a text at a lower point in the student's Lexile range. Throughout the period, teachers can compare the material the student has read, as well as her performance with that material, to the Lexile goals they set, to determine if the student is on track or whether the goals may need to be adjusted. At the end of the period, a review of the material and Lexile range the student has experienced will remove any question as to whether the stated goals have been met.

Another useful tool in this kind of systemic reading program will be the kind of reading logs and reading portfolios that you may already be using to assess student reading. Using Lexiles to record the student's reading achievement, the recommended readability level of texts the student may wish to try, and the challenge presented by the books the student has read, can provide a level of accountability to your assessment and permit the student to develop a sense of self-direction and mastery as she sets her own goals and monitors her progress toward them. It can also aid in explaining the student's progress to parents, and in providing the teacher an overall assessment of the effectiveness of the teacher's reading program.

The Lexile Framework can provide even more useful information when the teacher goes beyond observing the individual student to tracking the needs of reading groups or of the entire class. For example, by averaging the Lexile measures of the members of her reading groups, the teacher will have a valuable guide to selecting appropriate books for the classroom library. This information can also provide useful feedback to the school librarian or media coordinator, feedback that will help him develop a school collection that adequately meets the reading needs and abilities of the student body.

This last point demonstrates another key element of the Lexile Framework: Lexiles can help educators communicate with one another, facilitating educator teamwork.

The Lexile Framework can enable classroom teachers to provide information that will help the librarian guide a student to productive reading experiences; team teachers to compare notes about a student's progress; all teachers to talk about strategies for student guidance; faculties to analyze their teaching effectiveness and set goals.

By using the Lexile Framework as a standard method of measuring reading ability and text difficulty, educators will undoubtedly find many ways in which the common language that the Lexile Framework provides can help them work together more productively to facilitate student reading growth.

The following examples demonstrate how the Lexile Framework can be implemented as part of a district- or school-wide reading initiative.

River City School District The focus of the district's reading initiative is to improve reading comprehension skills by requiring students to read at least 30 minutes per day. In addition, the district stated that they wanted students to focus on books that would help improve their reading comprehension skills. To implement this goal, the district decided to incorporate the Lexile Framework into their comprehensive reading program.

The plan began with the administration of a test that could also be reported in Lexiles in order to obtain Lexile measures for all of the students. The school board also decided that for a textbook to be included on the district-level textbook adoption list, the textbook had to have a Lexile measure. Teachers then spent time examining the relationship between the reading levels of their students and the reading demands placed on the students by the textbooks they were using. Armed with this information, the teachers were better able to determine which students needed additional support with textbook assignments. The teachers also identified trade books across a range of Lexile measures that could be used in science and social studies to support the material in the textbooks.

River City Elementary School At this school within the district, students were required to read at least five books at their target level during each nine-week grading period and to read at least ten books at their target level during the summer. The media centers in each school spent the time and resources to put the Lexile measure on each of their books, while at the same time maintaining their current organizational structure. Books had to have Lexile measures in order to be on the school's recommended reading list, which contained at least 25 titles for each 100-Lexile range of student measures. The lists were developed by the teachers in the school based on the criteria that the books be developmentally appropriate for the various grade levels and support the district-wide curriculum. Members of the Parent-Teacher Organization also reviewed the reading lists.

Group Reading and Guided Reading

Especially in the primary grades, the reading group based on student skill levels is a standard part of the reading program. The challenge to the teacher in making these groups work successfully is to find ways to group students by ability, and to provide each group with the text materials that will meet their developmental needs. Many teachers are routinely presented with a wide range of reading abilities within any one class. In addition, they may be uncertain about the text difficulty of the vast number of new books released each month. The result is that teachers often use a narrow range of books, such as the leveled vocabulary of the basal reader.

As with the other targeting challenges we've discussed, the Lexile Framework can help with both parts of this process, removing the guesswork from establishing reading ranges and text levels for the groups.

Teachers can assess the reading competency of individual students with much more precision, and establish groups in more flexible and creative ways. Lexiles also free the reading group from the predictable leveling of basals, allowing teachers to present a wider range of literature.

In the intermediate and middle school grades, students are often assigned to reading classes based on ability; the class novel, which many students read and discuss together, becomes the signature method in such classes. Again, awareness of the Lexile measures of both students and texts will help make class assignments easier and more productive.

A popular new form of the reading group is found in the guided reading method as described by Fountas and Pinnel (1996). In guided reading, teachers use dynamic grouping to assign students to reading groups; the groups are reformed often as students develop and their needs change. In each session, the students have copies of the same text, which has been leveled to fit their reading abilities. The teacher may begin the session by briefly providing some background on the text, or discussing vocabulary or concepts that may prove challenging. Next, the students read the assigned text passage silently. When they are finished, they discuss with their group what they have read. The teacher may also ask students to read passages aloud. Throughout the discussion, the teacher makes careful observations and records what she learns in running records she keeps for each student.

Guided reading is popular because of the flexibility of the grouping method, which also avoids the stigma that students can experience from continually being in the "low group." Teachers also like its focus on real texts, group discussion, and authentic assessment techniques. The drawback to guided reading is that the process of managing continually-shifting groups, finding adequately-leveled materials, and keeping individual running records presents a tremendous workload for the teacher who wishes to use the method conscientiously.

The use of the Lexile Framework can ease this workload considerably. As with traditional reading groups, Lexiles make the process of student assignment easier. The 75 percent rule which is a part of the Lexile Framework helps teachers translate the miscue analysis they perform in the group setting directly into adjustments for text difficulty. And Lexile leveling of texts decreases teachers' reliance on books that have been leveled with a variety of different readability formulas—or from having to level the books themselves. The common, absolute reader-text scale of the Lexile Framework can prove useful in negotiating the many text matching decisions that guided reading calls for.

Special Reading Programs

Text matching becomes an even greater challenge in remedial reading programs and enrichment programs for gifted students. Students are often assigned to these programs because of their scores on standardized reading assessments. Test scores by themselves provide little help when matching students with texts or communicating with students and parents about the student's needs. When tests are linked to the Lexile Framework, however, teachers have a rich criterion-referenced interpretive frame for standardized assessments. It is much easier to explain how well a student is reading when it can be done in terms of everyday books. For example, if Sam scored a 150 on the district's fifth-grade standardized reading assessment, his teacher can relate this score to how well he should be able to read *Beethoven Lives Upstairs* (750L) by Barbara Nichol.

In these special programs, creating positive and rewarding reading experiences is even more challenging. Students are generally assigned to remedial programs in grades 3 and beyond, at the point at which most of their peers have developed adequate reading skills. They may already have developed negative attitudes about reading that will impede their progress; and as reading becomes more central to learning in the coming years, students who falter at this point may find themselves falling farther and farther behind in all subjects. Gifted students have different needs, but their situation is much the same; unless teachers keep them adequately challenged, they can easily become bored and distracted, fail to become engaged with school as a resource for learning, and end up as students who fall short of their potential.

Students in both programs need reading to become a "flow" experience, in which they can feel a sense of mastery and growth. The use of the Lexile Framework to track the ability level of these students and match them with texts that can provide the appropriate balance of success and challenge provides a number of benefits to both teachers and students. The problem of translating between test scores and readability formulas is eliminated, and both remedial and gifted students can explore a wider universe of text materials as a result. Occasional informal assessments using Lexile benchmark texts provides teachers in either program with ongoing guidance as to each student's ever-changing developmental achievements and needs. Communication between teacher and student is greatly enhanced: Remedial students are not stigmatized by the negative associations of grade-equivalent leveling, and false expectations about the abilities of gifted students are less likely to develop. In either remedial or enrichment programs, Lexiles take the guesswork out of matching reading test scores with readability of texts.

Home Reading/Summer Reading Programs

Increasingly, teachers are attempting to help students extend and consolidate the reading gains they've made in the classroom by encouraging students to continue their reading at home. Various methods for motivating and guiding parents to read to and with children are used, as are summer reading programs, often held in cooperation with local public libraries.

The Lexile Framework provides an easily-understood basis of communication with parents that avoids the inferred value judgments of grade leveling. It permits the teacher to generate reading lists that help parents guide their children to appropriate reading experiences, and helps keep the school and public library in synch when planning summer reading programs.

As an aid in developing reading lists, MetaMetrics, Inc. has developed Reading Pathfinder and Subject Pathfinder Lists. Individual Pathfinder Lists consist of 50 fiction and nonfiction selections and have been developed for each 100-Lexile segment of the Lexile scale. In addition, these lists provide a general guide to the age appropriateness of specific titles by noting whether the materials are intended for elementary (E), middle (M), or high (H) school students. The Subject Pathfinder Lists consists of thematically grouped titles along with a summary of each book. The titles on these lists have been chosen from lists published by the American Library Association, the International Reading Association, Reading is Fundamental, The Children's Book Council, and The Center for the Book of the Library of Congress.

Conclusion

We hope our discussion in this chapter has demonstrated the great versatility of the Lexile Framework in its many applications to literacy education, both in the classroom and beyond. We have concentrated here on language arts instruction—Reading with a capital "R." However, reading plays a crucial educational role in content courses as well as the media center and the home. In the next chapters, we will explore in more detail the way that Lexiles can be used to help make reading a more successful experience for students in whatever setting they encounter text.

References

Chall, J. (1996). *Stages of reading development* (2nd ed.). Fort Worth, TX: Harcourt Brace and Co.

Fountas, I., & Pinnell, G. S. (1996). *Guided reading: Good first teaching for all children.* Portsmouth, NH: Heinemann.

Gray, W. (1925). *Twenty-Fourth Yearbook of the NSSE, Part I–Report of the National Committee on Reading.* Bloomington, IL: Public School Publishing Co.

Manzo, A. (1975). Guided reading procedure. *Journal of Reading,* 10, 287-291.

Chapter 6

Lexiles and Content Reading

Introduction

During the 1990s, the emphasis in reading instruction has been to "read across the content areas." Many standardized reading assessments have shifted to an emphasis on reading science and social studies selections rather than just fiction or biography selections. With this shift comes additional hurdles for the reader to overcome. Many of these texts, while developmentally appropriate based on their content, often contain material at a readability level beyond the reader's Lexile range. For example, these content-based texts often contain specialized vocabularies and explain complex concepts. To meet the diverse learning needs of students and content-area teaching goals, teachers need to be provided with guidelines for matching students with materials that meet their needs. In this chapter we will discuss how using the Lexile Framework can help to reinforce familiar content material and enhance the learning of new concepts. A method for analyzing the comprehension challenges imposed by content-area reading will also be described.

Using the Lexile Framework Throughout the Curriculum

The Lexile Framework is a useful tool for enabling concept development in reading across school subjects and grades. From their earliest reading experiences, children in the primary grades are already reading to learn new ideas and gain new understandings in all content areas, even as they are developing their fundamental reading skills. As students progress through school, their content reading load in science, social studies, and mathematical concepts increases dramatically in size, complexity, and difficulty. The Lexile scale directly ties student reading ability to text difficulty, enabling you to target reading assignments and content activities that are appropriate for your students.

A number of factors beyond text readability determine the level of reading challenge a student encounters with a text, and these factors are often intensified in content area reading. Students come to class with a unique history that defines their expectations about literacy. Their attitudes and expectations are conditioned by years of school reading experiences already before they open their first textbook in your content class. Based on these experiences, students' familiarity and interest with the subject matter at hand also have a strong influence on their ability to handle a particular text. This could potentially create a wide range of different reading vocabularies, which complicates the picture. To enable students with such diverse needs to learn from the same textbook, content teachers should examine students' range of prior knowledge and make adjustments as they target assigned content materials.

To encourage optimal progress with the use of any reading materials, content teachers need to be aware of the difficulty level of the text relative to the student's reading level. A text that is too difficult not only impairs the student's ability to learn from it, it also serves to undermine the student's confidence as a reader in general. A text that is too easy fosters unproductive work habits and unrealistic expectations, and can deter the academic success of even the best students.

The Lexile Framework provides a scale that helps teachers align text difficulty factors with students' reading abilities on an individual basis. This enables the teacher to individualize reading assignments as well as to group students for selected readings at their appropriate levels. The basic rule of thumb for matching students with other kinds of reading material applies in the content area as well: A student's Lexile measure represents the level at which that student can read with about 75 percent comprehension. This marks a range of difficulty that extends about 50 Lexiles above and 100 Lexiles below the student's Lexile measure. Reading above this range presents a level of difficulty that prevents the student from inferring meaning from the text. Conversely, texts below the student's reading range will not present enough challenge to the student and may lead to boredom and disengagement.

In general, assign texts at or below the student's Lexile measure when factors make the reading situation more challenging, threatening, or unfamiliar. Use texts at or above the student's Lexile measure to stimulate challenge and growth, or when you will be adding support such as teaching background concepts, pre-teaching vocabulary, or facilitating post-reading activities, such as reading discussion groups.

Of course, the classroom teacher often does not have the ability to select the textbook that will be used to teach a particular subject. Even if you cannot target the difficulty level of the text, however, knowing the gap between the optimal reading range of your students and the Lexile measure of the text will permit you to systematically target instruction that facilitates reading difficult text. In other words, the Lexile Framework allows you to systematically off-target students (i.e., reader measure exceeded by text measure) when you want to teach reading strategies for attacking difficult texts.

As you work with Lexiles, you will become more confident in your ability to use the Lexile scale to make appropriate adjustments in order to target text difficulty for different students and different situations. Using Lexiles, teachers can know the reading competency of individual students with much more precision, and establish content reading assignments in more flexible and creative ways. Equally importantly, by using the Lexile Framework, the teacher can determine whether or not the content to be learned matches the students' reading abilities, and if not, how much additional teacher support is necessary for content learning to take place.

Determining the Match Between Students and Textbooks

Whether you are targeting a text to students or off-targeting students to a text, you must begin by knowing the students' individual Lexile measures, and the Lexiled readability measure of the content materials you wish to assign.

Begin by obtaining the Lexile measures for the texts you wish to assign. An increasing number of textbook publishers are including Lexile measures for their books, and Lexile measures are available for periodical articles and supplemental materials as well. Rank the materials you wish to assign by Lexile measure. Finally, write down the current Lexile measures for your students, again ranking them by Lexile measure. Compare the ranges of the text Lexile measures to the student measures. How well do they correspond? You can repeat this exercise with any core or supplemental reading material.

Content Textbooks

Teachers are well aware of the differences that their students bring with them as they go about their content work. While no one can change past histories, the teacher can still make adaptations to optimize content learning. Teachers can find ways to adapt the classroom learning environment to compensate for lack of prior knowledge by using multimedia, supplemental materials, nonfiction trade titles, visiting speakers, and instructional strategies for supporting reading. These adaptations will be especially necessary if there is a gap between student reading ability and the readability of the course textbook.

Content teachers are familiar with the warning, "Don't teach to the text!" Yet the reality is that a clearly written, easy to understand textbook provides structure, uniformity, and many of the relevant details for class units and lessons. Consequently, many teachers are likely to guide their students through a course of study using one primary textbook, but taking the responsibility for how it is used and what other reading materials will supplement it. By and large, good teachers use the textbook, but are not limited or controlled by it.

The extent to which a textbook will be a useful instructional tool depends on whether students will be able to read and understand it. Indeed, textbooks were not always written with regard to readability. Since the mid-1970s, this has all changed. For example, it is possible to find American History textbooks at many different reading levels, from upper elementary through advanced placement levels. Now it is possible to identify textbooks that more appropriately match the needs of your students through your district's own textbook adoption process. But even if your textbook is an older one, and even if you feel that it isn't exactly the right one for the level of your students, you are faced with the same problem as those teachers who have the luxury of choosing their own textbook: One size doesn't fit all!

Rather than shying away from assigning difficult reading, or from relying on reading assignments for instruction, it is important that students spend time with difficult materials (Fielding & Roller, 1992). When students have supported interactions with difficult content, their content knowledge increases, which may help make future tasks easier. Conversing with teachers and peers as they attempt to negotiate difficult texts will increase their content knowledge as well.

There are many methods the teacher may use to prepare students for reading the textbook itself and for understanding its concepts. One often overlooked—but very effective—method is called the teacher read aloud with commentary (Vacca & Vacca, 1986).

Teacher Read Aloud with Commentary

Because it is easier to listen than to read, learners understand new material better when they use their listening vocabularies. The teacher read aloud with commentary method works like this: The teacher selects a section of the textbook, either one that is hard to understand or one that is essential content for the course. Then the teacher reads the section aloud to the entire class. Some students may follow along in their textbooks. Others may simply listen to the teacher reading. The teacher may prompt the students with an initial question before the reading begins. After beginning, however, the teacher remains focused on the text and content, not pausing to ask any questions or to answer any student questions.

While reading, the only time the teacher pauses is to make comments about the material, selecting hard words to explain or new concepts to relate. The commentary is more of a conversation about the text, a "think-aloud" if you will. This method works best if kept short—about ten minutes or so. Since students learn vocabulary and concepts very well this way, teachers can also use this method with newspaper and magazine articles or other ancillary materials.

When the read aloud is finished, there are a variety of ways to consolidate learning. Some teachers have the students open their learning logs and write down the significant information that they learned. Younger students can draw a picture. At times, the teacher might try using a focused cloze procedure, taking a portion of the actual text that was read, deleting certain words, and having students fill in the blanks. This is a good way to build new vocabulary words and new concepts.

KWL

The KWL method is designed to enable active reading of textbooks and other nonfiction materials (Carr and Ogle, 1987). This strategy consists of constructing a three-column grid with students. The three columns are titled Know, Want to Know, and Learned. Before reading, discuss the material with your students, first asking what they know, or think they know. Enter their answers in the first column. Then, as other questions surface from the students, consider also what your students do not yet know, but want to learn. Enter these questions in the second column.

Next, have your students read the text. After reading, discuss the KWL grid again with them, having them complete the third column by summarizing what they have learned from the reading. Once you construct a basic KWL grid, you can then expand it during the course of your lesson. For instance, you may wish to categorize all the information on the grid, building a topical outline of the content. Or, you may wish to have students conduct further investigations on some of their questions that were not answered in the materials. This simple strategy is itself effective in preparing students for actively reading their assignments.

Content Area Vocabularies

A primary reason why content textbooks are so challenging to read is their heavy vocabulary load. New words and concepts increase the difficulty of the text significantly, leading to student confusion and frustration. It is important to analyze the vocabulary challenges presented by textbook reading, and to adapt the instructional setting to support students' comprehension.

Textbook vocabularies are comprised of three distinct kinds of difficult words: 1) technical vocabulary words, 2) specialized vocabulary words, and 3) unique words that are simply unfamiliar to students.

Technical vocabulary words are words that are unique to a particular content field of study. What distinguishes technical vocabulary is that its meaning is associated only with the content of the specific subject matter being studied, which limits the student's ability to bring past vocabulary skills to bear in constructing meaning.

Specialized vocabulary words present a similar challenge, with an interesting twist. Specialized vocabulary words carry specific technical meanings in the context of the subject, but also have wider, more general meanings as well. The words may look familiar to the reader, but without specific content background, the meaning is lost. For example, the word "plot" means something quite different in mathematics and language arts classes.

Other words are simply unfamiliar words, not necessarily having technical or specialized meanings, but words that are unknown to most students. In any extended text, some words are always anaphora, or terms that can only be understood by referring to the context. Mature readers can usually pick up many unfamiliar word meanings as they read in context. Developing readers are not always so skilled, nor do they have the background knowledge.

For the developing reader, then, the thousands of new words encountered in content reading presents a primary learning challenge. Consequently, students need not only to recognize technical vocabulary in print; they need to understand the concepts surrounding each new technical term.

The sight word technique (Cunningham, 1995), familiar to primary reading teachers, is an appropriate method for associating sounded and written words, then rehearsing the words until they become automatic. The association process begins by finding a synonym for the new word. Students begin to learn words for which they have a concept, and an oral vocabulary synonym or equivalent (for example, to "heave" means to "throw").

Two other strategies content teachers may borrow from the primary classroom to assist in vocabulary development are decoding by analogy and structural analysis. Decoding by analogy is the process whereby a child figures out how to pronounce a word by thinking of another word similar in appearance (Cunningham, 1995). Structural analysis refers to breaking down compound words into their roots, prefixes, and suffixes. The pieces are sounded out, then reassembled back into the whole word. This strategy is useful for deciphering the word's meaning as well as its pronunciation.

Teaching new words representing known concepts can be done by taking a list of difficult words, then constructing a sentence using each word, along with clear context clues as to its meaning. Providing a definition with a sentence reinforces the word's meaning. Another method is to write a paragraph that incorporates the selected word repeatedly, in different contexts.

Finally, using the dictionary to define words is an invaluable tool for learning words. However, young readers need to have dictionaries appropriate to their developmental level, along with instruction on how to use them correctly.

Handling Content Density and Concept Overload

Concepts are abstract terms or generalized ideas that contain sets of supporting ideas. New concepts frequently coincide with new words, as well as with meanings that increasingly involve subtlety. A unique feature of content textbooks is that they are almost always densely loaded with new concepts. One team of researchers, Lloyd and Mitchell (1989) found that in a single chemistry text, there were 67 new concepts presented in all of nine pages!

Lloyd and Mitchell's study demonstrates the importance of analyzing the content density of textbook and supplemental reading assignments. Their three research questions are the same questions content teachers need to consider when planning instruction:

- How important is the concept to the curriculum?
- How completely is the concept developed in the text?

- What level of prior knowledge do students need in order to be able to understand the concept?

These questions provide a simple model to use to analyze your classroom materials. First ask, "Is this an important concept for students to know?" If the answer to this question is "no", then don't teach it. If the answer is "yes", the next step is to determine whether the concept is covered clearly and sufficiently in the text. If so, you may rely on the textbook as long as it matches students' Lexile ranges. If the concept is not covered clearly and thoroughly in the text, then you will need to support the textbook with additional instruction. Finally, consider what prior knowledge and background students have with the concept. If some students understand it, they may help others to understand through classroom discussion, cooperative group learning, or other student-to-student interaction. If, however, the concept is completely foreign to the class, then plan to build background knowledge as you teach the concept more fully.

Reading Beyond the Textbook

Most teachers rely on a primary textbook for much of their content instruction. As we've discussed, however, there are problems with relying on the textbook as a sole source of content. Readability levels, content density, technical vocabulary, outdated material, clarity of writing presentation, and depth of explanation can hinder students' ability to learn from the text. In addition, their lack of interest in reading the textbook, their lack of background knowledge to understand it, or their inability to read the text itself may also hinder their ability to learn from the text.

The content teacher can circumvent these potential problems by relying more on supplemental materials for instruction. In addition to the more common supplements (newspapers and magazines to update students with current information), researchers strongly recommend using literature—novels, biographies, autobiographies, storybooks, and other works of fiction and nonfiction—throughout the curriculum (Anderson, 1996).

Often referred to as trade books, both nonfiction literature and historical fiction books provide students with a compelling foundation for complex concept development. For example, reading Stephen Crane's *The Red Badge of Courage* can provide the kind of indelible picture of the human cost of the Civil War that may be hard to find in a textbook. Supplemental reading assignments can be a pleasant way for students to reinforce the concepts they've been introduced to though textbooks and other instructional activities. And trade book reading can help address the challenge presented by the wide range of reading abilities among students in the average classroom. By preparing a selection of trade books at a variety of difficulty levels, teachers will have the materials necessary to guide students to reading experiences that are appropriately targeted to their comprehension needs.

The student engagement and concept reinforcement that free reading in content-related literature can provide has encouraged many content teachers to include sustained silent reading of topic-appropriate titles as a regular part of instruction. Using the Lexile Framework to target such reading for students will make this activity even more productive.

Conclusion

There is simply no substitute for textbooks and other written study materials as instructional tools in the content classroom, especially as students progress in the grades. Not only is reading the most time-effective way of teaching advanced concepts, reading empowers studentsas well to explore beyond the limitations imposed by oral presentation, and prepares them to use literacy as a lifelong learning skill. These benefits are too important to dispose of simply because we find ourselves in the unfortunate position of having textbooks and other materials that students cannot use successfully without help. The Lexile Framework can help by giving teachers a means to match the text to the reading range of the students in their classes; and when reading levels cannot be targeted, Lexile measures help us understand the discrepancy between student comprehension skills and text difficulty, so that we can better plan to support difficult texts with a variety of scaffolding and reinforcement activities.

References

Anders, P. (1993). Using interactive teaching and learning strategies to promote text comprehension and content learning for students with learning disabilities. *International Journal of Disability, Development, and Education,* 39 (3), 224-238.

Anderson, R. (1996). Research foundations to support wide reading. In V. Greaney (Ed.), *Promoting reading in developing countries.* New York: International Reading Association.

Carr, E., & Ogle, D. (1987). KWL Plus: A strategy for comprehension and summarization. *Journal of Reading,* 37, 626-631.

Chambliss, M., & Calfee, R. (1998). *Textbooks for learning.* Malden, MA: Blackwell Publishers.

Cunningham, P. (1995). *Phonics they use: words for reading and writing* (2nd ed.). New York: HarperCollins.

Fielding, L.,& Roller, C. (1992). Making difficult books accessible and easy books acceptable. *The Reading Teacher,* 45, 9.

Herber, H., & Herber, J. (1993). *Teaching in content areas with reading, writing, and reasoning.* Boston: Allyn and Bacon.

Lloyd, C., and Mitchell, J. (1989). Coping with too many concepts in science texts. *Journal of Reading,* 32 (6), 542-545.

Nagy, W., Anderson, R., & Herman, P. (1987). Learned word meanings from context during normal reading. *American Educational Research Journal,* 24, 237-270.

Nagy, W., Winsor, P., Osborn, J., & O'Flahavan, J. (1994). Structural analysis: some guidelines for instruction. In F. Lehr and J. Osborn (Eds.), *Reading, Language, and Literacy* (pp. 45-58). Hillsdale, NJ: Erlbaum.

Pittelman, S., Heimlich, J., Berglund, R., & French, M. (1991). *Semantic feature analysis: classroom applications.* Newark, DE: International Reading Association.

Ryder, R., & Graves, M. (1998). *Reading and learning in content areas.* Upper Saddle River, NJ: Prentice Hall.

Schwartz, R., & Raphael, T. (1985). Concept of definition: A key to improving students' vocabulary. *The Reading Teacher,* 39, 676-682.

Vacca, R., & Vacca, J. (1986). *Content area reading.* Boston: Little, Brown.

White, T., Sowell, J., & Yanagihara, A. (1989). Teaching elementary students to use word-part cues. *The Reading Teacher,* 42, 302-308.

CHAPTER 7

LEXILES IN THE MEDIA CENTER

Introduction

In a growing number of schools, the media center—or school library, if you prefer—has been transformed from simply a resource to the center of literacy education in the school. Librarians and media specialists have fully embraced their role as teachers, and are assuming a greater responsibility for creating a rich reading environment for students, not only in the library but throughout the school.

We believe media specialists will find the Lexile Framework an important asset in helping them play their central role in reading education. As we have discussed, the Lexile Framework is a tool that can be used to help guide students to appropriate reading experiences. This has long been a primary responsibility for school librarians as they aid students wandering the stacks. The common scale provided by the Lexile Framework can improve communication between the classroom and the media center, making it easier for media specialists to combine their observations with those of classroom teachers and other reading educators, increasing the multiple indicators that lead to a rich, performance-based assessment of student reading ability. In addition, by offering a useful method of indicating the readability of texts, the Lexile Framework can help make the library more accessible to students, and empower them to play a more self-directed role in their own reading development.

In this chapter, we'll suggest some methods for adapting library collections in order to utilize the Lexile Framework, and discuss how librarians and media specialists can use this important tool to help maximize reading success for their students.

Targeting Students in the Media Center

The same targeting procedures we discussed in Chapter 3 work as well in the media center as they do in the classroom. If students have been using Lexiles to discuss their goals and progress with their classroom teachers, they should be familiar enough with their Lexile range to provide that information to the media specialist along with other selection criteria when they ask for help in selecting a book. If the student's Lexile measure is not readily available, the informal assessment techniques we suggested in Chapter 3 will help the media specialist quickly zero in on the appropriate reading range for a student.

Many media specialists are spending more time in classrooms, helping to develop classroom book collections and working in partnership with classroom teachers. Media Specialists and classroom teachers should certainly devise communication strategies that help them successfully target readers using the Lexile Framework. The classroom teacher can provide information about the Lexile ranges of individual students and classes; in turn, the media specialist can research and provide materials the teacher may need to assist in targeting reading to students. As media specialists collaborate with teachers to develop special collections to support class reading assignments, reference to the Lexile measures of both students and texts will help insure that the readability of the selections will be appropriate. The teacher and media specialist may also collaborate on intervention strategies for students who require extra guidance and assistance in trying to attain their reading goals.

Being able to search, sort, and select from a collection based on Lexile measure is an important capability for media specialists who wish to use Lexiles to facilitate targeted reading. Fortunately, the Machine Readable Cataloging (MARC) records system, developed by the Library of Congress and included in most automated library systems, includes a field for readability levels, and Lexile measures can be entered in that field in place of grade-equivalent leveling. You can read more about "Field 521-TARGET AUDIENCE NOTE (R)" at the MARC web site, http://lcweb.loc.gov/marc/marc.html. Performing this kind of update by hand can be a time-consuming task, but many of the major school book publishers and distributors are including Lexile measures as part of the information they provide for their books, and there are MARC processing firms that can provide mass updates of your records. Speak to the company that supplied your library automation software about the best way to upgrade your system.

Once you have this information in your system, you will be able to produce customized reading lists for students based on their appropriate Lexile ranges, along with their other interests or reading needs. Remember to use the targeting techniques we discussed in Chapters 5 and 6 to modulate reading difficulty for the various purpose and context factors involved in the student's book search.

Book Labeling

One way to assist students in identifying books that will meet their comprehension needs is to label books with their Lexile measures. Labeling will help students find books of interest at appropriate reading levels, thereby promoting their use of media center materials. As students are aware of their own Lexile reading ranges, it will be important to provide this information on individual books and periodicals. This will allow them to apply their metacognitive awareness to the selection process, along with other motivating factors such as author, genre, information needs, and so on. Book labeling empowers students to control the challenge presented by the reading material they select, thereby providing a sense of self-determination, which can be a powerful motivator for many students.

Many librarians and media specialists are wary of labeling books. For one thing, the process of creating, applying, and maintaining book labels can be tremendously labor-intensive. Beyond the effort involved, however, librarians often are concerned that labeling books can be a barrier to intellectual freedom for students. They are concerned that a book label may have the effect of discouraging children by suggesting that certain books are "off limits" to them. Certainly, obvious marking of the exterior of books with grade levels can be detrimental for older students with less developed reading skills, who worry about being seen selecting and reading "baby books." When this happens, book labeling can hurt the very students it is most intended to help.

We believe Lexile labeling, if it is done sensitively and appropriately, overcomes many of the concerns engendered by grade-level labeling. Exterior labeling, as well as segregating and shelving materials by reading level, is a practice that should be avoided for all but the very youngest readers, for whom the traditional colored dots can be an important aid. Instead, a small label in the bottom corner of the inside front or back cover bearing the Lexile measure for the book or periodical is a sufficient way to provide this information for students. By removing the pejorative connotations of grade leveling, Lexile labeling takes the focus away from how the student compares with his or her peers, and returns it to the level of challenge afforded by the text in question. Rather than restricting access, Lexile labeling empowers the student to explore topics, authors, and genres with the confidence that his or her selection will provide a successful reading experience.

As for the labor of labeling books, many automated collection systems, as well as the Scholastic Reading Counts! reading management program, have the capacity to print labels for books, and can be adapted to provide the Lexile measure as part of the process. Find a few student and parent volunteers, and your labeling project is well on its way to completion.

Collection Development

Another way the Lexile Framework can be useful for media specialists lies in its potential to help develop the media center's collection at appropriate reading levels for the student population. With the reading specialist's help, the media specialist can compare student Lexile levels with the Lexile levels of books and periodicals in her collection. In this way, the media specialist can analyze how well her current supply of reading materials fits the comprehension needs of the student body.

The importance of collection readability has long been a concern of librarians and media specialists, because they readily see which books are read avidly and which are ignored. Media specialists who use the Lexile Framework find that it can be an accurate and flexible tool for analyzing and developing the readability of their collections to more fully meet the needs of all of their students.

The librarian can begin with the results of a school-wide reading assessment reported in Lexiles. Rather than simply focusing on averages, a distribution curve of assessment results can be a revealing portrait of the varying reading ranges of the school population as a whole. As with most distribution curves, the reading assessment is likely to present the typical bell-shaped curve.

If the media specialist is fortunate enough to have access to an automated library record system that has had Lexile measures added to it, it should then be relatively easy to sort the collection by 50L increments, and produce another distribution curve that shows what percentage of the collection is at any given 50L segment of the Lexile range. The use of a computer spreadsheet program to calculate percentages and draw diagrams can make the process easier. To make the process easier initially, you may wish to begin with an analysis of subsections of the collection—fiction, nonfiction, content areas, reference materials, and so on—before performing an analysis of the whole collection.

This process will produce two distribution curves, one for students and one for books, with a common Lexile scale at the bottom. By comparing the two distribution curves, it can become visually apparent how well the school's library collection matches the comprehension needs of the student body. Both curves will likely have bell shapes: Where the center and ends of those curves fall on the Lexile scale reveal much about how well the collection is matched to students. If the center line of the curve is shifted farther to the right than the student Lexile curve, it may indicate that the collection as a whole may be too challenging for many readers—a common situation in schools with populations that tend to have reading problems. Conversely, if the center line of the collection is shifted to the left of the center line for the student curve, the collection may not provide enough challenge to foster reading motivation and development.

As important as the centers of the curves are the distributions on either end. Students with below-average reading ability especially require reading materials that promote a sense of mastery and success. On the other side of the scale, above-average readers need a level of reading challenge that keeps them from becoming bored and disengaged and fosters their reading development as well. If the percentage of students at either of these ends is significantly greater than the proportion of library collection within their appropriate Lexile range, it may be a sign that the collection is not meeting the special needs of these students.

As you conduct this kind of analysis, it is important to remember that a student's Lexile measure describes the center of a range of appropriate reading materials, from easier books for leisure reading to more challenging material for study and exploration. A well-rounded collection will contain material both below the bottom end of the student distribution curve, as well as above the top end, in appropriate proportions as suggested by the distribution of the student Lexile measures. The information this analysis provides can be a useful guide in making acquisitions of new materials, permitting you to bolster your collection in any area where you have determined that it may not be meeting student needs. It can also serve as powerful documentation of the need for additional resources to build your collection.

Conclusion

The changing role of the media center from a place where books are housed to an extension of the classroom has opened up the world of books to reading for a variety of purposes—for literary experience, to gain information, or to perform a task. Just as adults enjoy reading books they select themselves, so do students. Because there are so many books available on any given topic, the task of selecting the one book that matches the student's reading level can be daunting. Labeling books with their Lexile measure can help students select texts that will result in a positive reading experience. These self-directed learners exhibit a desire to learn for a lifetime, acquire the competence to learn in real-life situations, and are motivated to produce quality work and products.

References

Pearson, R. (1999). *The school library media specialist's tool kit*. Fort Atkinson, WI: Highsmith Press.

CHAPTER 8

USING LEXILES WITH READING MANAGEMENT SYSTEMS

Introduction

A reading management system is a computerized system that uses quizzes to assess student comprehension of books and produces reports that provide educators with a variety of information about student reading performance. Over the last decade, reading management software programs have become popular with a growing number of teachers and media specialists. These educators believe that a reading management system can help motivate students to read and provide teachers with a tool for tracking and managing individualized reading programs (Engoall, 1999).

In this chapter, we will review the features of the most common reading management systems, and discuss how using the Lexile Framework in conjunction with reading management software programs can make this technology an even more effective tool for guiding student reading.

Overview of Reading Management Systems

While reading management software programs have grown in both number and sophistication since their initial appearance in the late 1980s, their basic characteristics have remained essentially the same. They consist of multiple-choice quizzes designed to assess whether students have read books with comprehension and recall. Students take these quizzes on a computer, which scores their responses and provides immediate feedback to students on their performance. The systems also award students with a certain number of points based on the length and difficulty of the book. These points can be used as the basis of extrinsic reading motivation activities.

Quizzes are generally available on a wide variety of fiction and nonfiction books. In addition, the systems permit users to author their own quizzes, generally within certain limits.

Reading management programs also produce on-screen and printable reports that provide teachers with a variety of information on student reading performance. These reports typically include the titles of the books students were tested on and the results of those tests, often along with information about the points assigned to the books, text difficulty levels, and the points students have earned. The reports can be produced for individual students; groups of students collected by class, reading group, or ability level; or for entire classes.

Initially, reading motivation systems became popular because students enjoyed taking the computerized quizzes. In addition, the incentive activities the programs facilitated encouraged students to read more books. However, teachers soon discovered that the information provided by these programs could be a useful tool in helping manage individualized student reading efforts. Compared with more traditional, labor-intensive assessments such as written book reports, the quizzes provide a greater level of assurance that students have actually read the books they claim to have read. By monitoring the reports carefully, teachers can identify which students are reading according to expectations and which might be in need of special intervention. These reports can also provide a convenient record of student reading, a record that is useful for discussing goals and achievement with students and parents, as well as helping students with book selections.

Software Review

The Accelerated Reader

Initially marketed under the name "Read-Up", the Accelerated Reader, published by Advantage Learning Systems, Inc., was the most widely used reading management program through the 1990s. Although neither the first nor the most sophisticated of these programs, its wide acceptance makes it a useful basis of comparison.

As of this writing, the Accelerated Reader (AR) offers quizzes on more than 25,000 fiction and nonfiction titles. Quizzes typically present five or ten multiple-choice items, each with four possible responses. The system can be set to produce a report each time a student passes a quiz that documents the student's results as well as the title and difficulty level of the book. Each book in the AR collection is assigned a set point value, based on a formula that considers the book's length and readability level. Printed reports include both individual and cumulative information on student reading goals, test results, and reading levels. In addition, the reports describe whether the book was fiction or nonfiction and whether the book was read independently or as a read-aloud activity. Diagnostic codes identify readers who are not testing or performing at minimum levels compared to overall class performance.

While its widespread use has made it the standard for reading management programs, there are a number of drawbacks specific to AR. First, its exclusive use of grade-equivalent leveling as a basis for reporting limits its usefulness as a tool for assessment and book matching. This problem is compounded by the fact that AR has changed the readability formulas and methods it has used to set grade levels on books over the years, creating leveling inconsistencies within its collection of tests. While response presentation in AR quizzes is randomized, each student responds to the same items for each book quiz, making cheating a problem and limiting a student's ability to retake a quiz. The vast majority of AR quizzes contain only audit-level items; i.e., fact-based questions designed to show whether the student read the book, but of little use in stimulating higher-level thinking. There is also no provision for the teacher to customize such features as quiz length, passing score, and point level to take individual student needs into account.

The Electronic Bookshelf

The Electronic Bookshelf (EBS) was the first reading management program widely available, and continues to maintain a loyal following. It contains largely the same features as AR, with some notable distinctions. EBS quizzes provide three responses per item, but items are drawn from a randomized item bank for each book. This provides some protection against cheating and permits students to retake a quiz if they fail it the first time. The program is also highly customizable, allowing the teacher to adjust book point levels, quiz length, passing percentages, and retake procedures for each student. However, the process of assigning reading levels to books has changed over the years, so the program is of limited usefulness in accurately matching students with appropriately challenging books.

Reading Counts!

In 1998, Scholastic Inc. acquired EBS, and substantially upgraded its interface and features. The result was the release in 1999 of Scholastic Reading Counts! (SRC). While still relying on the multiple-choice quiz, SRC combines the four-response format with a randomized item bank for its quizzes. Quiz questions include inference and main idea questions in addition to basic recall. The program retains many of the customizing options of EBS, while maintaining a stable point structure for its books. Student responses to books are tracked, and they are included among more than 30 different reports SRC can create. The online search function includes summaries as well as author, genre, and readability information about the books in the quiz collection.

Most important from the standpoint of book matching, SRC includes book leveling in Lexiles in its reports, along with traditional grade leveling. In addition to providing the Lexile measures of student book selections and allowing users to search for books by Lexile measure, the program prints stickers that permits discrete labeling of books with their Lexile measures.

Online Reader

The most recent reading management program also uses Lexiles as its basic readability scale. EBSCO Publishing's Online Reader has many of the features of other computerized reading programs, but focuses on periodical articles instead of trade books. As with the other programs, students either select or are assigned articles from a library of 350 selections. A computerized quiz tests their comprehension of the article, and students are awarded points for successful completion of the test. Also unique to Online Reader is that its item bank includes cloze and sentence completion items in addition to multiple-choice items. Teachers can use the student's Lexile range to assign articles or guide students to appropriate selections. As with EBS and SRC, there is a fair degree of adaptability to the program, with features that let the teacher customize tests and point values to the needs of their students. Online Reader should be a welcome addition for teachers who wish to extend the benefits of reading management software beyond the realm of trade books.

Using Lexiles with Reading Management Systems

Reading management systems can be an important ally in using Lexiles to guide student reading choices. By providing a current assessment of student success with specific texts, reading management systems provide teachers with immediate and ongoing feedback about student reading performance. When this assessment is combined with the use of the Lexile Framework, teachers have a dynamic information tool that helps them track student progress and guide student reading choices.

Teachers using Scholastic Reading Counts! or EBSCO Publishing's Online Reader will have little difficulty applying Lexile leveling to their efforts. Reports will give them the Lexile measures of the books students have tested successfully on, as well as those they have struggled with. The program's search function will allow the teacher to combine the student's Lexile range with student interests in authors, topics, or genres to create customized reading lists that guide students to books they should be able to read successfully and enjoy.

Although it will require a little extra effort, classrooms that use other reading management systems will find that these also can be powerful tools for implementing Lexile-based student reading guidance. What follows is a list of suggestions for using Lexiles with reading management systems that do not report results in Lexiles.

Basic Procedure

Begin by determining each student's Lexile measure using the methods discussed in Chapter 3. Use this measure to suggest books from the program's quiz list that are in the appropriate Lexile range for the student. When the student completes the book, he or she takes the computerized quiz on that selection.

If the student is able to answer at least 75 to 80 percent of the questions on the quiz correctly, chances are good that the book was within the student's competency range. In this case, the student should be encouraged to select more books within the range. If the student failed to respond with a minimum of 75 percent accuracy, the teacher should intervene with the student to determine whether the book was too difficult, or whether some other factor may have affected the student's performance. Similarly, if the student scores 100 percent on a quiz, especially if he or she does so consistently, it may well be time to encourage the student to attempt more challenging reading.

If you informally determined the student's Lexile measure, the student's results on the quiz will help you verify whether that initial Lexile determination was reliable. If the student is unable to answer 50 percent of the quiz questions correctly or answers all of the questions correctly, it may be necessary to adjust the student's Lexile range downward or upward to provide more successful reading experiences.

As you can see, the ongoing use of computer quizzes to assess reading success with particular texts fits in well with the multiple-indicator model of assessment that the Lexile Framework was designed to facilitate. It is possible that a variety of factors besides reading comprehension may contribute to determining how well a student does on any given quiz. When quiz scores from a number of books are tracked over time, however, the increasing amount of data produces a more accurate and reliable picture of student ability and growth. This picture is dynamic as well, permitting teachers to intervene effectively as student needs change, without the need for continual read-aloud checks or other time-consuming assessments. By incorporating the Lexile Framework into a reading management system, much of the guesswork and inaccuracy inherent in grade-equivalent text leveling is removed.

Adapting Reports to Lexiles

Grade leveling in reading management reports creates a bit more of a challenge. Reading management reports still provide you with a great deal of useful information about student reading behavior—what books students are reading, and how many; what their performance rate is on quizzes; and even a rough approximation of reading levels. Yet reading levels are still based on flawed grade-leveling methods, as are point-level assignments for books in some instances.

The best alternative is to use the other kinds of information available on the reports, and make notations of Lexile text measures at appropriate times. For example, just as you include test result reports in a student portfolio, you can document the benchmark texts students have read successfully by noting the Lexile measures. This would be especially appropriate for quizzes on texts you used to reconfirm or adjust the Lexile reading range you recommend to the student. When it's time to review a student's progress, the Lexile measures of the books will then be available along with the standardized documentation of the student's efforts.

Conclusion

Reading management systems provide a number of benefits, not the least of which is a series of multiple indicators of reading achievement and growth. Teachers who wish to implement the Lexile Framework, especially those in districts and states that have adopted the framework as their official measure of reading comprehension, should find Scholastic Reading Counts! and EBSCO Publishing's Online Reader to be useful tools for making Lexiles a daily element of their reading program. However, any reading management product can be used to provide the evidence of student achievement with individual texts and, when calibrated with the Lexile scale, can become a powerful instrument in tracking and fostering reading growth.

References

Engvall, B. (1999) *The carrot to read: Computerized reading incentive programs.* Library Talk, November/December, 25-30.

Scholastic, Inc. (1999). *Scholastic Reading Inventory Interactive*: Educator's guide. New York: Scholastic, Inc.

Chapter 9

Using Lexiles to Communicate with Parents and the Community

Introduction

As we have observed in a number of contexts, one of the benefits of the Lexile Framework is its capacity to provide a common language with which to discuss student reading needs and progress. One of the most important applications of this common language can be in communicating with parents and caretakers, as well as with the general public, about their children's reading progress.

In this chapter, we will discuss the importance of educating parents and the community at large about the use of Lexiles. We will also share some tips for communicating these efforts directly to parents, and for communicating through the media, open-house occasions, and presentations to community groups.

Communicating with Parents

A notable advantage of using the Lexile Framework over traditional grade-leveled reports of reading ability is that we can avoid stigmatizing students based on implied comparisons with their peers. As we have discussed, grade-leveling depends on norm-referenced assessments that can be tenuous at best, especially if they are based on personal observations of student success with grade-leveled texts rather than standardized tests. Furthermore, while grade leveling is based on derived statistics of a wide range of student scores, the resulting levels imply that all students at a certain age would be expected to perform at the same level. This is an unrealistic expectation that is bound to lead to disappointment for the parent whose fifth grader reads at a "3.6 grade level." Even the parent who is gratified by hearing that her third grader reads at a fifth-grade level is being misled as to what this really means about the child's abilities and progress. The Lexile scale's absolute metric for students is based not on other children, but on textual difficulty. This removes the distraction of peer comparison and makes it easier to focus on what each child can read.

This direct connection of student reading abilities to real, specific texts makes The Lexile Framework an excellent tool for communicating with parents about reading. As we will discuss in Chapter 10 on standard setting, no longer must we rely on general language, couched in the specialized language of reading professionals, to talk about what our expectations are for student reading. The Lexile Framework provides a way to move beyond the confusing and often misleading interpretations of norm-referenced test scores. The Lexile Framework has the capability to communicate to parents the reading ability of their students and how it is changing. When standards and scores are reportable in Lexiles, it is easy to provide examples of student goals or achievements by converting the Lexile measure into a range of specific, familiar texts. When we think of how much more useful it is to be able to tell parents whether their third graders are ready for fourth-grade textbooks, or if their graduating seniors can read and understand a newspaper, a job application, or a college entrance exam, the communication potential of the Lexile Framework becomes clear.

Techniques for Parent Communications

Home Reading Programs

Reading at home is important to students' overall reading growth and development. Teachers in primary grades increasingly communicate with the home in order to encourage and document student reading outside school. The Lexile Framework can be a useful addition to these activities.

Teachers may consider developing a reading folder that goes home with students and comes back weekly for review. The folder can contain a reading list of books within the student's Lexile range that are also appropriate for the student's interests. Reports of any recent assessments (in Lexiles)—anything from informal reading inventories to standardized tests, can be incorporated. Another possibility is to include a form for parents to record the reading that occurs at home, both aloud with parents and for students' independent reading. A home reading folder can encourage parents to play a more active role in their children's reading development and to pay more attention to what, and how often, their children are reading. The inclusion of Lexile measures for students and books adds extra benefit to the reading folder by giving parents a useful way of monitoring the level of reading challenge presented by read-aloud activities as well as independent reading at home.

One of the items that should be included in the home reading folder is a sheet that provides a simple explanation of the Lexile Framework and how it applies to the texts students will encounter at school. In addition to a written explanation that the Lexile measures refer to the difficulty of the text, a graphic scale covering the range of material appropriate to your grade, and key texts as reference points on the scale should all be included. An example of how such a scale might look in a typical fourth-grade classroom is shown below:

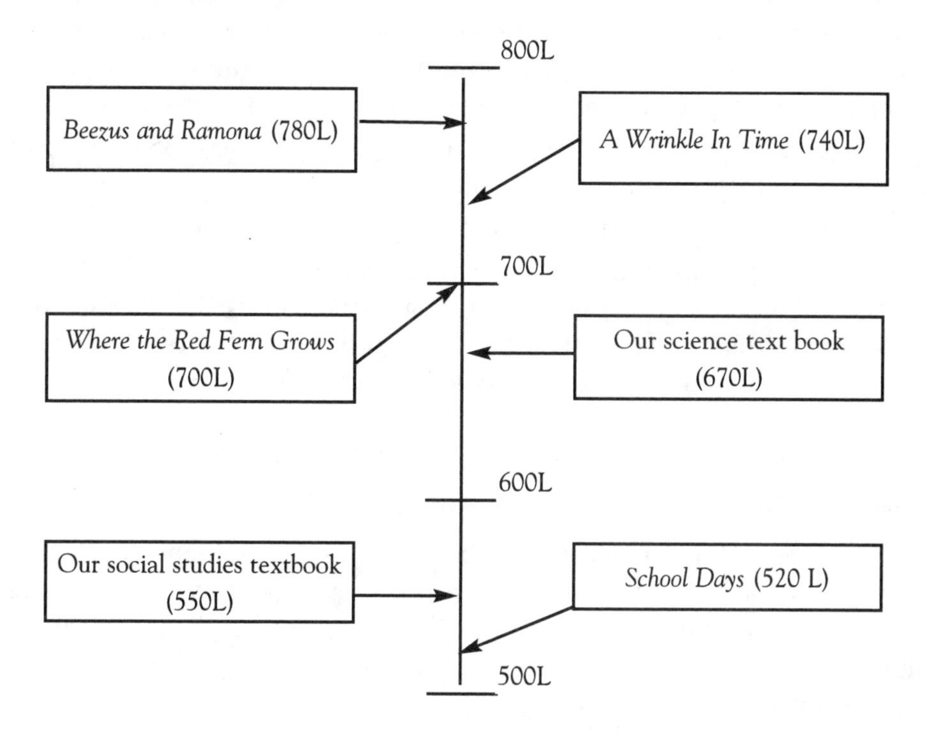

By giving parents a graphic representation of the Lexile range of texts their children will encounter, they will both understand how the Lexile Framework functions and have a sense of how their child's current reading comprehension skills fit with the kinds of reading they actually have to do in school. This kind of concrete, text-based communication makes it much easier for parents to understand student needs and goals.

Portfolios

Another commonly-used method to communicate with parents about student reading progress is the reading portfolio, a record of books a student has read within a given period. A reading portfolio may include a written record of titles, student writing or other response projects related to books they've read, and documentation of any reading assessments that have been conducted, such as reading inventories or the results of reading management system quizzes.

The Lexile Framework helps reading portfolios do a better job at their central task, which is to document student progress based on performance with actual texts. This can be accomplished by recording the Lexile measure of each book included in the student's portfolio, as well as including Lexile reports for any other reading assessments the student completes. The reports produced by computerized reading management systems are excellent documentation to use for this purpose (see Chapter 8 for our discussion of reading management systems).

As parents review their child's reading portfolio, Lexiles provide them with an easy way to understand their child's reading ability and accomplishments in a way that is grounded in actual texts. Portfolios allow parents to review multiple indicators of their child's reading comprehension, both documenting the student's appropriate Lexile range and giving a tangible demonstration of growth and progress throughout the year. A copy of the Lexile information should be included, to provide an explanation of the Lexile scale for parents as they review the portfolio.

Open House

One of the best ways to introduce both parents and community members at large to the Lexile Framework is to make it a focus of a special open house. This presents an opportunity to speak personally with attendees and show them how reading materials in classrooms and the media center and have been selected and organized.

A major feature of an open house chould be a series of bulletin-board or poster-board displays that show both the grade-appropriate Lexile range and examples of specific texts that relate to the Lexile scale. A typical display for a fifth-grade classroom might have a yardstick type scale drawn down the center from top to bottom, calibrated and labeled with the Lexile range from 700L to 1000L (in much the same way as graphic on the Lexile information sheet was drawn). Titles of typical texts to be used in that class—articles, textbooks, basal readers, trade books, and other instructional materials—should be placed according to their Lexile measure on either side of the scale. In addition, samples of the texts, book covers, photocopies or drawings from the texts could also be included. If appropriate, the scale could also be marked with goals or standards specific to the reading program at that grade level.

Information can be displayed in the library and media center, as well as classrooms, to show how Lexiles are used both in collection development and to help students locate books within their Lexile reading ranges. Examples of texts at various levels can be displayed and labeled with their Lexile measures, so that visitors can examine them and get a practical sense as to how the reading challenge of a text varies with its Lexile measure.

Finally, a take-home sheet can be distributed that briefly explains the Lexile Framework and how it is used. Be sure to include the various Lexile ranges appropriate for each grade, and use specific texts to illustrate the kind of reading materials the range represents. You should also indicate whether specific standards or goals have been set in Lexiles, and whether Lexile reporting will be a feature of tests or other reading assessments.

Report Cards

A district may choose to adopt the Lexile Framework and to include the student's Lexile measure on his or her report card. While this is certainly a valid way to communicate with parents, it's important that the Lexile measure be properly explained and grounded in familiar texts. Along with the Lexile measure, an information sheet similar to the one we suggest for home reading folders should be included. If possible, the child's Lexile measure should be referenced to corresponding texts. For instance, you might note that a child's 950L measure indicates he or she can read *The Secret Garden*, or that the student can comprehend the science or math textbook reading assigned to him or her. Without this kind of preparation, parents will view the Lexile measure as yet another mysterious label that has been applied to their child, and will be unable to take full advantage of what this number can tell them about the child's reading ability.

Community Outreach

Why It's Important

Reading is one of the core skills that is expected to be taught at school. As a result, student reading ability is one of the chief factors people examine when they assess the quality of schools. The announcement of the results from the most recent state reading exam never fails to excite the interest of the media, and to be quoted everywhere from the newspaper letters column to the television campaign advertisement. Any educators who have had to survive the furor when reading test scores go down can attest to the fact that many people in your community pay careful attention to reading scores.

The impact of poor results on high-stakes reading tests can be wide-ranging: from throwing teacher competency into question to threatening school budgets. In some states, schools can face severe disciplinary action if test scores decline consistently. Conversely, schools that are perceived as teaching reading well may become the center of grateful attention by a community which values what good education can do for everything from property values to economic development efforts.

In light of our discussion about the usefulness of traditional metrics for measuring reading performance, the weight the public places on test scores should be disturbing to educators. We often hear outrage that scores are below the national average, or that a certain percentage of students read below grade level, without any recognition that these factors may tell us quite little about the actual reading capacity of students. Certainly, this reproach seldom sheds much light on the question of what student reading skills ought to be, or what we can do to insure that students can read up to the standards we set for them.

The growing importance placed on high-stakes reading tests is one of the reasons a growing number of states have sought more useful means for measuring and/or communicating student reading performance—and why they have turned to The Lexile Framework as tool to help them achieve those goals. Yet it is not enough for educators to adopt a more useful reading metric for themselves and their students alone. If the public is not educated about the Lexile Framework and its use, we cannot take advantage of the benefits Lexiles may provide in helping the community understand the true state of literacy education in our schools. If your school, district or state has adopted the Lexile Framework, you will benefit most if you take steps to insure that the community is aware of your initiative and understands the Lexile measures they see on test results and report cards. Failure to do so may mean that, rather than adding clarity, your use of the Lexile Framework will simply add confusion to public understanding of literacy education. On the other hand, public awareness of the Lexile Framework can help community members gain a greater understanding of reading standards and reading test results, and assist community decision makers in playing a greater partnership role in the effort.

Suggestions for Community Awareness Activities

Raising public awareness of the Lexile Framework need not be an overwhelming source of additional work. It can simply be a matter of making sure Lexile information is an ongoing part of your public outreach activities, and that you take advantage of opportunities to communicate to a wider audience.

Community Relationships A way to involve the community in your reading initiative is to work with public libraries and bookstores when reading lists are developed. As an example, bookstores can be approached by the school district for support as they began their adoption of the Lexile Framework. The bookstores can be urged to stock books the schools have included in their initiative, and display them prominently along with their Lexile measures.

Media Relations News and other information media are an important resource for helping community members understand your reading initiative and how the Lexile Framework plays a role in it. Certainly, the results of high-stakes tests will be reported there. If your district or state is using Lexile reporting as a part of such tests, it is important that the news media be informed about what Lexiles mean and how they should be used.

You may wish to issue a press release early in the program—perhaps at the beginning of the semester in which your school, district, or state adopts the Lexile Framework. Because it marks the start of something new, and because reporters are aware of the keen interest parents take in test scores, you should find it relatively easy to use this opportunity to help everyone understand the new reporting system. Holding an open house in conjunction with the beginning of your program, or incorporating Lexiles into a regularly-scheduled event, will provide additional incentive for the news media to cover the story, as well as a chanceto illustrate the advantages of this tool for your students.

It would probably be wise to have a statement available that defines Lexiles and details how your school uses them to determine reading standards and benchmarks, as well as how they apply to assessments of student reading. Such a one- or two-page statement should be distributed to faculty and staff, and kept on file, ready when you need it.

Follow-up contact with the media should take place whenever you have a development in your reading program: the establishment of new standards or reading techniques; additions to your library or media center collection; the release of the results of high-stakes test scores. Each of these opportunities gives you a chance to translate news about student reading from the rather mystifying argot of quartiles, stanines, and percentages into terms that reporters and community members understand: Namely, the texts students can actually read and use.

Be certain to use references to real texts every time you communicate through the media about goals, standards, benchmarks, or test results. For example, in addition to reporting that 45 percent of your eighth graders read above 1100L, put this number in perspective by adding that it indicates those students are capable of reading the average newspaper or computer instruction manual.

Service Group Presentations One low-cost and relatively easy way to reach a large number of influential people in your community is to prepare a presentation for service groups such as Kiwanis, Rotarians, Optimists, etc. These groups are continually in search of speakers for their meetings, and are quite interested in education issues. A 15-minute presentation on your school's Lexile initiative, including the kinds of graphic explanatory materials we've discussed in this chapter, should be well-received by local service groups. This presentation will help you inform opinion leaders in your community about Lexiles, and may serve as the basis for developing supportive partnerships with the organizations and their members.

Business Partnerships It may also be a worthwhile effort to approach business leaders in your community to ask for their support. Business people are keenly aware of the importance of literacy education, and are often interested in becoming involved with literacy programs. Certainly, if your Lexiled standards for student reading are tied to texts students will need to read in the workplace, business people in your community will be interested in your efforts.

Conclusion

No school stands alone. It is vitally connected with the parents of its students and with everyone in the wider community who depend on the school's success and on whom in turn the school depends for its success. Since reading is a major component and indicator of the success of a school, it is important that schools take advantage of the communications potential the Lexile Framework presents to insure that parents and community members are aware of and can participate in the school's reading success.

References

Baker, L. (1999). Opportunities at home and in the community that foster reading engagement. In J. Guthrie & D. Alverman (Eds.), *Engaged reading: Processes, practices and policy implications*. New York: Teachers College Press.

Hall, S., & Moats, L. (1999). *Straight talk about reading: How parents can make a difference during the early years*. Chicago: Contemporary Books.

Levin, I., & Levin, M. (1998). *Read to me! Read to me! A guide to reading children's literature aloud*. Westminster, CA: Teacher Created Materials.

McCarthey, S. J. (1997). Connecting school literacy practices in classrooms with diverse populations. *Journal of Literacy Research*, 29, 145-182.

Serpell, R., Sonnenschein, S., Baker, L., Hill, S., Goddard-Truitt, V., & Danseco, E. (1997). *Parental ideas about development and socialization of children on the threshold of schooling (Research Report No. 78)*. Athens, GA: Universities of Georgia and Maryland, National Reading Research Center.

Snow, C., Burns, S., & Griffin, P. (1998). *Preventing reading difficulties in young children*. Washington, D.C.: National Academy Press.

CHAPTER 10

STANDARD SETTING WITH LEXILES

Introduction

The standards movement is perhaps the most far-ranging and sustained effort related to school reform in the past century. As Richard F. Elmore, a professor at Harvard University's graduate school of education, observed, "Accountability for student performance is one of the two or three—if not the most—prominent issues in policy at the state and local levels right now" (Olsen, 1999). Based on the survey conducted as part of Quality Counts '99, 48 states now test their students, and 36 publish annual report cards on individual schools. The 1998 National Assessment of Educational Progress (NAEP) reading assessment results for grade 4 found that "states deeply involved in the so-called systemic reform model that has gathered momentum during the 1990s showed consistent and large gains from 1992 to 1998." In response to these results, Secretary of Education Richard Riley concluded that "states that have taken the lead at standards-based reform are getting the good results" (Hoff and Manzo, 1999). From the U. S. Secretary of Education to nearly every village school board, the effort to determine clear standards for what our children should know and be able to do has become an all-consuming task. It has often been an acrimonious and controversial task as well, especially as we attempt to find language to describe our expectations for students, and, by extension, for our teachers.

Reading and the language arts have certainly been no less challenging than any other area of standard setting; and from our discussion of the difficulty of quantifying student reading ability, it's not hard to understand why our efforts to set standards and benchmarks for reading have been marked by confusion and contention. A brief look at the history of setting reading standards will help cast some light on our current problem.

What is a Standard?

To begin with, we must step back and define our terms. What do we mean when we say we want to set a standard?

A useful definition is that a standard is a statement about what is valued that can be used for making a judgment of quality (NCDPI, 1999). Speed limits, height and weight tables, and daily recommended nutrition allowances are three examples of standards we encounter every day.

We notice that with each of these examples, our standards are relative to characteristics that are measured on some scale. Speed limits are set in miles per hour; height and weight tables are set in inches and pounds; and the recommended daily allowance (RDA) is set in percent per serving.

We can also observe that standards in all three areas have changed over time. We reset the speed limit on freeways from 55 to 65 mph; the optimal weight for your height changes as we learn more about health; and the RDA for any nutrient changes as we learn more about nutrition. However, the basic metric stays the same: speed limits may vary, but they are always expressed in miles per hour.

From these examples, we can observe that standards involve:

- A scale for measurement; and
- A line on that scale that indicates a goal or expectation.

A growing trend in education is to differentiate between content standards (curricular frameworks that specify what should be taught at each grade level) and performance standards—what students must do to demonstrate various levels of proficiency with respect to the specific content. Increasingly, educators and parents want to know more than just how a student's performance compares with that of other students: of growing interest is "What level of performance does a score represent?" and "How good is good enough?"

For any test scale a number of points can be identified that correspond to a specified level of performance. For example, on the National Assessment of Education Progress three levels of performance are identified: basic, proficient, and advanced. Proficient achievement on the NAEP reading assessment is defined as "solid academic performance for each grade assessed. Students reaching this level have demonstrated competency over challenging subject matter, including subject-matter knowledge, application of such knowledge to real-world situations, and analytical skills appropriate to the subject matter" (NAGB, 1999).

The History of Standard Setting

An understanding of how standards work gives us a useful context to examine the way educational standard setting has changed over the course of the last 30 years.

In the 1970s, school districts tended to rank order students in order to determine who would be required to take remedial courses during the summer. A district might determine that a certain percentage of students at the bottom of the scale would qualify for summer school. This percentage was often based on the resources of the district: How many of its lowest-performing students could it afford to send to summer school? There are some benefits of setting a standard in this way. For example, school districts have a limited amount of resources, so this kind of standard setting was a practical way of spending the money on those who may have needed it the most.

In the late 1970s and early 1980s, standard setting became more norm-referenced. For example, students could be eligible for educational interventions if they scored in the lower quartile on standardized achievement tests. Among other things, norm-referencing led to what we might call the "Lake Woebegone effect," in which over time, most districts were able to show that nearly all their children were "above average." Still, the method was another way to set the line with a metric. Percentile results from standardized tests were the metric, and quartiles were the lines.

By the mid 1980s, standard setting began using a benchmark strategy, where the goal was to have students achieve at certain specified levels or demonstrate specific competencies. This performance benchmarking is the hallmark of standard setting today, the arguments centering on what kinds of benchmarks make sense at what educational level. Often, the benchmarks are defined by target scores on criterion-referenced tests.

If you are interested in learning more about standard setting, refer to *Handbook for the Development of Performance Standards* (1998) prepared for the U.S. Department of Education and The Council of Chief State School Officers by Linda N. Hansche. This document is available online from The Council of Chief State School Officers (www.ccsso.org).

The problems with most educational standard setting methods are evident if we remember our everyday examples of standards. We set speed limits based on our needs for safety, fuel conservation, and convenience. We don't set them based on how fast all the cars on the road are going at any given time. Yet, instead of setting reading standards based on what students need to be able to read, we have set them based on their test scores. Indeed, only in education do standards seem to be unrelated to the larger context of why we need standards in the first place. No wonder it has been so challenging for us to answer what might seem like a simple question: What should our students be able to read?

Using Lexiles to Set Standards

There are two basic advantages to using the Lexile Framework as a basis for setting reading standards:

- First, Lexiles are not linked to a specific test, but can be derived from any standardized test. The standards you establish in Lexiles, then, are not dependent on the test you use, but are instead based on student reading ability based on texts. This kind of instrument-free standard setting prevails in other areas of life—imagine if every car speedometer measured speed differently! It's time for instrument-free standards in education, too.
- Secondly, you can now have multiple indicators report a common metric. Instead of only one annual measurement of student ability, you can now compile a variety of measurements and observations, all convertible to the Lexile scale: standardized tests, informal inventories, student reading portfolios, and teacher observations. The more information you have, the more accurate your assessment can be. The Lexile Framework allows you to aggregate measurements and observations that could not be combined before.

In sum, the Lexile Framework provides a text-based metric that allows us to incorporate multiple indicators to track student ability and development.

A Model for Developing Standards

Rather than struggling over abstract definitions of optimal student reading performance, using the Lexile Framework for standard setting allows us to ask relatively simple and straightforward text-based questions that quickly clear up ambiguities about our expectations.

Let's imagine a committee formed to set standards for fourth-grade readers. The main question before the committee can now become, what should fourth graders be able to read? The language arts teacher on the committee may have benchmark books to put on the list—say, *Where the Red Fern Grows* or *A Wrinkle in Time*. The science and social studies teachers will want students to be able to read the assigned text books with enough comprehension to complete and learn from their reading.

By examining the Lexile measures for all the books on the committee's list, it would quickly become apparent what range of reading abilities was required of fourth graders. Those expectations could in turn be expressed as a numerical range that would encompass any text a teacher wanted to use, and many assessments for determining ability and progress. For fourth graders, that range tends to fall between 500L and 850L. So our committee could express the standard for fourth-grade readers at some point in this range, depending on the outcomes they want their standard to promote. This process should be repeated with another committee to ensure the consistency (reliability) of the standards that are defined.

As standards are set from one grade level to the next, certain issues surface. First is the issue of articulation. The fifth grade needs to be higher than the fourth and so on. Secondly, we have to determine the appropriate range of growth throughout the grades. All of these decisions can be facilitated by asking ourselves the ultimate question: What do we want our ultimate end-product to be? What should high school students be able to read when they leave school?

This question can be answered in a text-specific way as well. We teach students to read in the first place because we want them to be able to use reading successfully as a skill they can apply to their lives. Our end-point standards, then, should involve texts that people need to read with enough comprehension to function in various areas of life. We could define five such basic areas of literacy:

- Workplace literacy
- Citizenship literacy
- Continuing Education literacy
- Moral/Ethical/Religious literacy
- Recreational literacy

Once again, by looking at benchmark texts in each of these areas, we can define a Lexile range for necessary competency. The range for the kinds of texts we encounter at work—training manuals, software documentation, and the like—tends to be about 1100L to1400L. To fulfill the obligations of an informed citizen, people need to read newspapers, which are typically written at the 1200L to 1400L levels. People who continue their education at community colleges or as university freshmen will encounter textbooks at an 1100L to 1400L range. The sacred books of the five major religions are written in a range between 1400L to 1600L. Finally, many popular novels and other recreational reading for adults range from 900L to 1000L—a Stephen King novel like *Pet Sematary*, for example.

With these Lexile measurements in mind, it's clear to see that high school graduates need to read at least at the 1100L to 1200L range to handle the texts they'll encounter as workers and citizens. Reflecting on the implications of this—that Dickens, Thoreau, and a Supreme Court decision should not be too much for the average high school graduate to comprehend—we are able to see that competency standards, especially minimum competency standards, we have set in the past may not have been adequate to our students' real-life needs.

By extension, then, we can create overlapping and interrelated standards for each grade level. At the top is our end-product goal: a metric based on actual texts we want high school graduates to be able to read. With a greater proportion of growth in the early primary grades and benchmark texts to calibrate growth throughout the grades, our standards will refer to specific textual accomplishments. No more semantic debates about reading goals. And, as we will see in the next section, no more confusion over how to tell whether students are accomplishing the goals we set out for them. Using the Lexile Framework to set standards has an important by-product: It allows us to set benchmarks that can be easily related to our standards.

Lexile Measures as Benchmarks

If our hypothetical committee were to set the standard that a student should be able to read at a level of at least 750L when he or she leaves fourth grade, the process of setting benchmarks to measure how far students have to go to reach the goal, and how adequate their progress is as they are developing, becomes much more straightforward. The previous year-end standardized test results, reportable in Lexiles, will give fourth-grade teachers an excellent starting point when the school year begins. And our district will know what percentage of its student population is not achieving expected progress and requires intervention.

As teachers record the books students read, the Lexile measures for those books become part of the benchmark evaluation as well. It will be evident that a student who has read *Henry and Beezus*, a Beverly Cleary book at 730L, is well on the way to meeting the fourth-grade standard. At the same time, a fourth-grader who has difficulty with Donald J. Sobol's *Encyclopedia*

Brown and the Case of the Sleeping Dog at 610L is going to need additional support.

Teachers can use Lexiles and specific Lexiled texts to help both students and their parents understand how the district's standards relate to the reading development and needs of each child. A growing number of districts are finding the student's Lexile measure to be a meaningful and useful addition to report cards. Finally, year-end test results and Lexile measures (auxiliary scores) allow each teacher and the district as a whole to judge progress toward the standards, and use that judgment to modify teaching strategies for the future.

While it should be clear that stating standards and benchmarks in Lexiles presents a number of distinct advantages, there are some crucial precautions we need to make. While each student will have a Lexile measure, we have to remember that that measure represents a point within their range of reading capability. A student's actual performance will vary within this range, due to all of the various factors of reader, text, and context we have discussed, including measurement error. Despite our temptation to use the Lexile measure as a kind of "mark on the doorframe," the kind we use to keep track of a child's height, we must avoid using Lexiles to label students in a way that prevents us from understanding the full range of their abilities. In our culture, numbers tend to acquire a power of their own—especially numbers expressed in district reading standards and report cards. It's important that we continually remind ourselves that Lexiles are designed to describe what a student can read—not to prescribe what they must read.

Lexile measures should be used as benchmarks and standards, not replacing existing standards, but supplementing them with clear Lexile data. A single Lexile measure should be used only for benchmarking reading progress over time. For example, you can compare Sara's Lexile measure in September with her measure at the end of each term and at the end of the year, to see that her reading ability is growing as it should. But for any reading lesson or independent reading activity, you need to remember that the student's functional reading level is a range as large as several hundred Lexiles, all of which is going to depend upon the reader, the text, and the context.

Conclusion

By grounding the process of standards and benchmark setting in the context of real texts we want our students to comprehend, and by providing us with an absolute scale on which to place both students and texts of any kind, the Lexile Framework provides a strong foundation for setting reading standards. As we have discussed, much of the confusion and resistance that has resulted from the establishment of performance standards is due to the lack of clarity of the end result (criterion) that we value, and the lack of a metric (developmental scale) that can identify where a student is and how far he or she has to go. The Lexile Framework goes a long way toward solving these problems, and should prove a useful tool, both for those who set reading standards as well as the teachers and students who must realize them.

References

Doyle, D., & Pimentel, S. (1999). *Raising the standard: An eight-step action guide for schools and communities* (2nd ed.). Thousand Oaks, CA: Corwin Press.

Education Week. (1999). Quality Counts '99: Executive Summary—Demanding results. *Education Week on the WEB,* 18 (17), 5. URL:www.edweek.org/sreports/qc99/exsum.htm.

Hoff, D.J., & Manzo, K.K. (1999). States committeed to standards reforms reap NAEP gains. *Education Week on the WEB,* 18 (26), 1, 12-13.

Idol, L., Nevin, A., & Paolucci-Whitcomb, P. (1999). *Models of curriculum-based assessment: A blueprint for learning* (3rd ed.). Austin, TX: Pro-Ed.

National Assessment Governing Board (NAGB). (1999). *Achievement levels.* Washington, D.C.: Author. URL: www.nagb.org.

North Carolina Department of Public Instruction (NCDPI). (1999). *Classroom assessment: Linking instruction and assessment.* Raleigh, NC: Author.

Olsen, L. (1999). Quality Counts '99: Shining a spotlight on results. *Education Week on the WEB,* 18 (17), 8. URL: www.edweek.org/sreports/qc99/ac/mc/mc-intro.htm.

Stenner, A. J. (1997). *The Lexile Framework: A map to higher levels of achievement.* Durham, NC: MetaMetrics. Inc.

Topolovac, E., Sammuli, M., & Smith, M. (1998). *Checkpoints for progress: In reading and writing for teachers and learning partners.* Washington, D.C.: United States Department of Education.

Zemelman, S., Daniels, H., & Hyde, A. (1998). *f4 Bestpractice: New standards for teaching and learning in America's schools.* Portsmouth, NH: Heinemann.

Appendix

Lexile Measures of Familiar Books

Title	Author	Lexile Measure
Wood and Other Materials	Hughes, Monica	90
Chairs, Chairs, Chairs!	Cappetta, Cynthia	100
Nate The Great	Sharmat, Marjorie	130
Fox on Wheels	Marshall, Edward	180
Happy Birthday, Ronald Morgan	Giff, Patricia	210
Snaggle Doodles #8	Giff, Patricia	260
Day the Teacher Went Bananas	Howe, James	310
Miss Nelson Is Back	Allard, Harry	320
Frog and Toad Together	Lobel, Arnold	330
Miss Nelson is Missing	Allard, Harry	340
Woodshed Mystery #7	Warner, Gertrude	360
Bony-Legs	Cole, Joanna	370
Peter's Chair	Keats, Ezra	390
Curious George	Rey, H.A.	400
Mike Mulligan and His Steam Shovel	Burton, Virginia	420
Can Do, Jenny Archer	Conford, Ellen	440
Schoolhouse Mystery #10	Warner, Gertrude	450
Danger Guys and the Golden Lizard	Abbott, Tony	460
Do Not Open	Turkle, Brinton	480
Pioneer Cat	Hooks, William	490
Magic School Bus Inside the Earth	Cole, Joanna	500

The Solid Gold Kid	Mazer, Norma & Harry	510
Ahyoka And the Talking Leaves:	Roop, Peter	520
The Giving Tree	Silverstein, Shel	530
The Rainbow Pony	Crompton, Anne	530
Herbie Jones and the Class Gift	Kline, Suzy	540
I'll Meet You at the Cucumbers	Moore, Lilian	550
Superfudge	Blume, Judy	560
Sarah, Plain and Tall	MacLachlan, Patricia	560
Hang a Thousand Trees With Ribbons	Rinaldi, Ann	560
The Whipping Boy	Fleischman, Sid	570
From Anna	Little, Jean	570
Stevie	Steptoe, John	580
The Magic Circle	Napoli, Donna Jo	580
The Pistachio Prescription	Danziger, Paula	600
After the Rain	Mazer, Norma	600
The Cat Ate My Gymsuit	Danziger, Paula	610
Phoenix Rising	Hesse, Karen	610
Fourth-Grade Celebrity	Giff, Patricia	620
The Good, the Bad and the Goofy	Scieszka, Jon	620
School's Out	Hurwitz, Johanna	620
The Secret of Sanctuary Island	Monson, A.M.	620
Homecoming	Voigt, Cynthia	630
Out of Control	Mazer, Norma	630
George's Marvelous Medicine	Dahl, Roald	640
Anastasia On Her Own	Lowry, Lois	640
Trout Summer	Conly, Jane	640
A Time for Dancing	Hurwin, Davida	640
In My Father's House	Rinaldi, Ann	640

The Not-So-Jolly Roger	Scieszka, Jon	650
Strawberry Girl	Lenski, Lois	650
A Case of Need	Crichton, Michael	650
Beauty	Wallace, Bill	660
Forbidden	Cooney, Caroline	660
Shadow of the Red Moon	Myers, Walter Dean	660
Class Clown	Hurwitz, Johanna	670
Walking Across Egypt	Edgerton, Clyde	670
The Cloud Book	De Paola, Tomie	680
Kid Power	Pfeffer, Susan Beth	680
The Eagle Has Flown	Higgins, Jack	680
The Day It Snowed Tortillas	Hayes, Joe	690
This Place Has No Atmosphere	Danziger, Paula	690
Kindertransport	Drucker, Olga	690
Anastasia Again!	Lowry, Lois	700
Where the Red Fern Grows	Rawls, Wilson	700
The Stalker	Nixon, Joan Lowery	700
Dicey's Song	Voigt, Cynthia	710
A Gown of Spanish Lace	Oke, Janette	710
Wolf-Speaker	Pierce, Tamora	710
The BFG	Dahl, Roald	720
On the Banks of Plum Creek	Wilder, Laura Ingalls	720
Eli and the Swamp Man	Sherman, Charlotte	720
Shadow Boxer	Lynch, Chris	720
Hello, My Name Is Scrambled Eggs	Gilson, Jamie	730
Water Sky	George, Jean Craighead	730
Chester Cricket's New Home	Selden, George	740
The Tower Treasure #1	Dixon, Franklin	740
The Cat Who Ate Danish Modern	Braun, Lilian	740

The 18th Emergency	Byars, Betsy	750
Misty of Chincoteague	Henry, Marguerite	750
Soup & Me	Peck, Robert	750
Kneeknock Rise	Babbitt, Natalie	760
Journey to Jo'burg: A South African Story	Naidoo, Beverley	760
The Case of the Daring Decoy	Gardner, Erle Stanley	760
The Chocolate Touch	Catling, Patrick	770
Have Space Suit-Will Travel	Heinlein, Robert A.	770
Stranger with My Face	Duncan, Lois	780
Mossflower	Jacques, Brian	780
Remember Me	Clark, Mary Higgins	790
Moon Dancer	Rostkowski, Margaret	790
Sweet Creek Holler	White, Ruth	790
The Whingdingdilly	Peet, Bill	800
Caught in the Act #2	Nixon, Joan Lowery	800
Ramona Forever	Cleary, Beverly	810
Summer of the Monkeys	Rawls, Wilson	810
A String in the Harp	Bond, Nancy	810
Carlota	O'Dell, Scott	810
Jupiter	Simon, Seymour	820
Farmer Boy	Wilder, Laura Ingalls	820
Shizuko's Daughter	Mori, Kyoko	820
Wizard at Large	Brooks, Terry	830
Acceptable Risk	Cook, Robin	830
Shadow of the Dragon	Garland, Sherry	840
Great Brain at the Academy	Fitzgerald, John	850
Julie of the Wolves	George, Jean Craighead	860
The Cat Who Went Into the Closet	Braun, Lilian	860

The Tangle Box	Brooks, Terry	870
Song of Solomon	Morrison, Toni	870
Brighty of the Grand Canyon	Henry, Marguerite	880
Stoner's Crossing	Pella, Judith	880
Pretend You Don't See Her	Clark, Mary	880
The Day of the Storm	Pilcher, Rosamunde	890
Having Our Say: The Delany Sisters' First 100 Years	Delany, Sarah	890
One Bird	Mori, Kyoko	890
Jean and Johnny	Cleary, Beverly	900
Last Stand at Papago Wells	L'Amour, Louis	900
Mama, I Want to Sing	Higginsen, Vy & Tonya Bolden	900
Dear Mr. Henshaw	Cleary, Beverly	910
Roll of Thunder, Hear My Cry	Taylor, Mildred	920
The Runaway Jury	Grisham, John	930
The Lion, the Witch and the Wardrobe	Lewis, C.S.	940
The Book of Ruth	Hamilton, Jane	950
The Shepherd of the Hills	Wright, Harold Bell	960
Wonderful Flight to the Mushroom Planet	Cameron, Eleanor	970
Show Boat	Ferber, Edna	980
Real Ponies Don't Go Oink!	McManus, Patrick F.	990
The Moon By Night	L'Engle, Madeleine	1000
Winds of Graystone Manor	Hoff, B.J.	1010
Frontier Lady	Pella, Judith	1020
Haveli	Staples, Suzanne	1030
The Girl Who Heard Dragons	McCaffrey, Anne	1040
A Stranger Came Ashore	Hunter, Mollie	1060
The Lottery Rose	Hunt, Irene	1070

The Power of One	Courtenay, Bryce	1080
Ferris Beach	McCorkle, Jill	1100
My Own Two Feet	Cleary, Beverly	1110
The Hero and the Crown	McKinley, Robin	1120
Winterdance: The Fine Madness of Running the Iditarod	Paulsen, Gary	1140
A Whole New Ball Game: Story of the All-American Girls Professional Baseball League	Macy, Sue	1160
Rebecca of Sunnybrook Farm	Wiggin, Kate	1190
Screwtape Letters	Lewis, C.S.	1250
A Brief History of Time (Updated Ed.)	Hawking, Stephen	1290
Our Country's Founders: A Book of Advice for Young People	Bennett, William J.	1300
The Marble Faun	Hawthorne, Nathaniel	1320
Power to the People: The Rise and Fall of the Black Panther Party	Hasking, Jim	1340
Brave New World Revisited	Huxley, Aldous	1360
Hillary Rodham Clinton	Kozar, Richard	1390
Walden	Thoreau, Henry David	1420
The Confessions of Nat Turner	Styron, William	1450
Justice at War	Irons, Peter	1470
A Fable	Faulkner, William	1520
Traitors	Pincher, Chapman	1590
Fundamental Principles of the Metaphysic of Morals	Kant, Immanuel	1620
The Principles of Scientific Management	Taylor, Frederick Winslow	1670
Discourse on the Method and Meditations on First Philosophy (Yale University Press, 1996)	Descartes, Renae	1720

INDEX

A

B

C

D

E

F

G

H

I

J

K

L

M

N

O

P

Q

R

S

T

U

V

W

NOTES

NOTES

NOTES

NOTES

NOTES

NOTES

NOTES

NOTES

NOTES